Stoicism for Beginners

How to Apply Ancient Stoic Wisdom Today using Practical and Simple Steps to Overcome Obstacles, Attain Contentment and Live a Better Life

Marcus T. Ryan

© **Copyright 2019 by Marcus T. Ryan - All rights reserved.**

The contents of this book may not be reproduced, duplicated or transmitted without direct written permission from the author.

Under no circumstances will any legal responsibility or blame be held against the publisher for any reparation, damages, or monetary loss due to the information herein, either directly or indirectly.

<u>Legal Notice:</u>

This book is copyright protected. This is only for personal use. You cannot amend, distribute, sell, use, quote or paraphrase any part or the content within this book without the consent of the author.

Disclaimer Notice:

Please note the information contained within this document is for educational and entertainment purposes only. Every attempt has been made to provide accurate, up to date and reliable complete information. No warranties of any kind are expressed or implied. Readers acknowledge that the author is not engaging in the rendering of legal, financial, medical or professional advice. The content of this book has been derived from various sources. Please consult a licensed professional before attempting any techniques outlined in this book.

By reading this document, the reader agrees that under no circumstances are is the author responsible for any losses, direct or indirect, which are incurred as a result of the use of information contained within this document, including, but not limited to, —errors, omissions, or inaccuracies.

Table of Contents

Introduction

Chapter One: How Stoicism Can Help You

Chapter Two: Ancient Greek and Roman Stoic Philosophy

Chapter Three: How to be a Stoic in Today's Fast-Paced World

Chapter Four: Applying the Stoic Teachings: Marcus Aurelius

Chapter Five: Applying the Stoic Teachings: Epictetus

Chapter Six: Applying the Stoic Teachings: Seneca

Chapter Seven: How to Deal with Negative Emotions

Chapter Eight: How to Thrive in a Stressful Environment

Chapter Nine: How to Apply Stoicism to Relationships

Bonus Chapter: Stoicism and Mindfulness
Conclusion

Introduction

Congratulations and thank you for owning Stoicism for beginners: *How to Apply Ancient Stoic Wisdom Today using Practical and Simple Steps to Overcome Obstacles, Attain Contentment and Live a Better Life.*

Our modern world is a fairly hedonistic one with moral relativism stretched beyond its own logical capacity present in lots of people. Stoicism can offer us a much-needed reaction against the problems of plenty that modern people face. While pleasure is one of the greatest parts of living, stoicism offers us meaning in life, which should always be prioritized above any sort of pleasure. Within this book, we will discuss ways in which to avoid falling into lots of the traps that many modern people find themselves falling into.

To this end, within this book we are going to discuss the topics of how stoicism can immediately help us. These topics are: Ancient Greek and Roman stoic philosophy, how to be a stoic in today's fast-paced world, the famous stoic philosophers Marcus Aurelius, Epictetus and Seneca. We will also discuss how to deal with negative emotions, how to thrive in a stressful environment, how to apply stoicism in relationships, and finally, a Bonus chapter on stoicism and mindfulness.

Stoicism often gets the wrongful reputation of a philosophy that teaches us to live without emotion. While this philosophy may teach us to curtail our lower passions, it still very much encourages us to experience our emotions to their fullest. There are many other books on the market on this subject, so it is appreciated that you have chosen this one.

Every effort was made to ensure that it is full of as much useful information as possible, so please enjoy!

Chapter 1: How Stoicism Can Help You

To begin our discussion of Stoicism, we should first start off with an accurate description of what stoicism is because it is all too often misrepresented today.

Stoicism is simply a certain school within Hellenistic philosophy founded in the 3rd century BC by the Greek philosopher Zeno of Citium. The school was originally heavily influenced by the teachings of Socrates and later independently developed its own system of logic which was then applied to real-life problems within the natural world.

One of the more primary and important tenets of stoic philosophy is the emphasis that it places on the present moment, that moment being the one thing that one should accept in order to find true happiness. There is also emphasis placed on not letting one's actions be determined by the desire for pleasure and or the fear of any pain. The Stoics also assert that one should apply one's mind to understanding the world better and to treating others both fairly and justly.

The Stoics were also revolutionary in their time in that they preached that the only good someone can possess is virtue, and that any other externalities, such as pleasure, wealth, and or health, were not necessarily good or bad in of themselves. These stoic ethics, along with Aristotelian ethics, form one of the strongest bases for modern western virtue ethics. As for negative emotions, the Stoics believed these to stem from only errors in judgment. They asserted that people should determine wills for themselves that are in accord with the happenings and affections of nature. Due to this fact, and like most moderns, the Stoics tended to judge people based less on what they said and more from how they behaved. Since everything was rooted in nature, the Stoics thought, it was necessary to understand the inner workings of nature.

The Stoics believed that virtue is enough cause for happiness, and therefore anyone who strived for the highest virtue would find lasting happiness and would be emotionally resilient in the face of any misfortunes. Therefore, it is only the sage from the Stoic view that would be considered true free among the people. Stoicism remained prevalent throughout the Greco-Roman world until the 4th century A.D. and one of its most famous adherents was the emperor Marcus Aurelius.

One common modern notion of stoicism that is out of line with the true nature of stoicism is the notion that practicing stoicism involves suppressing one's true emotions. This is divorced from the true nature of stoicism because a true stoic is genuinely indifferent to pleasure, fear, or pain. In other words, there is no repression of emotion necessary where indifference to the given emotions is already in practice.

Now we should discuss the potential benefits of learning more about stoicism. The first and perhaps most beneficial of these is the effect that the practice of stoicism can have on a person's emotional intelligence. Contrary to what popular modern conceptions of stoicism would have you believe, the art of practicing stoicism involves a great deal of emotional intelligence. When negative emotions are repressed without being properly examined and interpreted, they tend to have more detrimental and long-term impacts on a person's overall well-being.

The greatest thing that stoicism has to offer in the way of developing emotional intelligence is that it not only allows for but encourages the investigation into dramatic events in a person's life in order to ascertain why the emotions felt towards the event are felt. this is expressed accurately in one quote of the Stoic philosopher Epictetus: "Men are disturbed not by events, but by their opinions about events." It is all too often that our own presuppositions pertaining to the happenings of our lives cause us more suffering than the actual happenings themselves. Practicing stoicism is a great way to check these presuppositions wherever they may arrive and to adopt any of these which we may find to be faulty.

One of the most useful tools that the early stoic philosophers offered in the way of adjusting these presuppositions was the use of affirmations. Stoics always valued habit formation and this use of daily affirmations, which is still used in CBT by most patients, reflects on this fact.

Unlike CBT, however, stoic philosophizing is not disease oriented. When practicing stoic thought, you can allow yourself to feel whatever emotions that naturally come to you without giving yourself the impression that there is something wrong with you. The affirmations used in Stoic philosophy are not directives so much as they are suggestions. While stoic philosophy encourages and indifference to any and all emotions, it does not suggest that there is anything wrong with feeling these emotions. One Axiom that could describe this is that emotions are not right or wrong, they are only felt.

While stoicism is still practiced by many atheists, agnostics, and religiously unaffiliated people, many Christians view the stoic philosophy as a threat or as a rival to Christianity. This is averse to the nature of Christianity, which extols the virtue in finding wisdom wherever it can be found. Make no mistake that stoicism as a school is never lacking in wisdom and that the texts of the ancient stoic philosophers will remain relevant throughout all time.

Overall, the stoic philosophy can and will assist you in meeting whatever goals you have as far as your emotional intelligence is concerned. One of the most common issues that people are faced with psychologically, and that is often the aim of CBT, is that they are too agreeable and often put other people's needs before their own. The stoic philosophy places great emphasis on the indifference towards what others think, but also on the importance of understanding the workings of nature as a whole. Contrary to much public opinion, stoicism will help you connect with your innermost thoughts and feelings, rather than repress them.

Stoicism offers much more than just an increase in emotional intelligence. Some of the greatest virtues of the mind that stoicism offers, as put by Seneca, are freedom, loftiness, fearlessness, and steadfastness.

In addition to the virtues listed above, one other stoic philosopher, Marcus Aurelius, extols the virtue in consistently connecting oneself with the world around us. He once famously asserted that the world should be perceived by one optic that encompasses the whole and that everything that exists as part of the whole of the universe. All substance is, therefore, part of one infinite substance. Spinoza would later add to this idea that even finite substances are infinite because they are limited only by other substances of the same nature, making even them infinite. All things, therefore, become cooperating causes of all other things that exist, ourselves included. It is much easier to feel like you serve some sort of purpose when looking at the world through this optic, which makes you feel like you are part of something much larger than yourself, which you in fact are.

The next stoic virtue, this one extolled by Seneca, is to live in the present. This is a commonly used one in mindfulness training. Seneca asserts that happiness is best found in being content within the present moment and that apprehensive dependence on the happenings of the future should be avoided. The key theme here is fulfillment. Happiness lies in being fulfilled within the present moment.

Here again, virtue is highly valued, this time by the philosopher Epictetus. Like Hobbes after him, Epictetus proclaims that men deliberate their actions based on appetites and aversions, following their appetites and avoiding their aversions. Happiness is caused when a person has his or her appetites fulfilled and Epictetus asserts here that the only reliable way of fulfilling these appetites is by living a virtuous life and constantly moving forward towards perfection.

Another point, this one illustrated by Marcus Aurelius, is that one needs to harness the power of his or her thoughts in order to move forward. Aurelius was determined that the happiness of a person's life was dependent upon the quality of his or her thoughts. With that being said, every one of us can create either a hell or heaven for ourselves, as many contemporary philosophers often point out.

Another important virtue of stoic philosophy is closely related to the previous point made on the views that people take on things as opposed to their actual significance. This virtue is set forth by Epictetus and states that people should not be so quick as to get very worked up about certain things. Again, our perceptions of situations are often more destructive than are the situations in of themselves, so we would always be wise to avoid jumping to conclusions about things and getting prematurely upset regarding things that we have not analyzed thoroughly. Here again, Stoicism teaches something somewhat like skepticism in its searching for answers beyond what is immediately perceived.

Another axiom that should here be mentioned that also relates to a point previously mentioned is the axiom that a person should avoid caring about what others think of him or her excessively. This point has been made by nearly every philosopher since the birth of philosophy in some form or another, but Marcus Aurelius pointed out one of the most illuminating facts convincing us in the west to avoid wasting energy worrying about what others perceive us to be. He famously pointed out that it is always strange that while every person in the world puts his or herself before all others, no person usually puts his or her own opinions of his or herself before the opinions of others. In fact, it is our own opinions of ourselves which all too often take on a subordinate role compared to what others see in us, which is an absurd way to live with oneself. A good way to avoid concerning yourself with others think is to remind yourself constantly that other people are, for the most part, just thinking about their own self-interests and are usually not very interested in your greater happenings in the first place.

Musonius Rufus warns famously against not treating others with charity. He suggests that when people do not ever do anything for those around them the fate of ostracism, which is usually worse than loneliness, inevitably meets them. A good stoic is always ready at a moment's notice to lend a helping hand to anyone in need.

Again, Epictetus provides us with yet another stoic virtue, this one being our last: gratitude. It will always remain irrelevant how much you happen to have so long as you are not thankful for any of it. You could acquire $50,000 tomorrow and be just as miserable the next day if your outlook is poor to begin with. Conversely, you could lose everything that you have tomorrow and still be elated if you are maintaining a positive outlook on life. Epictetus' quote here is paraphrased as such: It is always much wiser to give thanks for the thing that you do have that to grieve over the things that you do not have. This takes on much of the tone of the first two revelations that Buddha came across: life is suffering, and the source of all suffering is wanting. Both the stoic and Buddhist philosophies preach that to avoid excessive suffering, it becomes necessary to release yourself of all the needless wants that you hold on to.

Most people mistakenly assume from some sort of heaven's gate fallacy that by releasing themselves of wants they will somehow be rewarded for the righteousness. This is rarely, if ever, the case though. True stoicism, as well as true Buddhism for that matter, teaches us that we need to genuinely avoid wanting things and that we should avoid backhandedly wanting things once we have been placed on the initial high horse that we find ourselves on after first proclaiming that we want not. With all this being said, stoicism (as well as Buddhism) may seem like a rather pessimistic philosophical structure to follow, but many would counter argue that stoicism is realistic above all else and is never marked by a shallow sophistication which prides itself on pessimism and cynicism, at least never in its purest form, that of the ancients.

Many of the basic axioms of ancient stoicism may seem like common knowledge today, but these ideas were revolutionary for their time. Not only that, but they hold true in every age and will probably always be considered more or less true as they are ingrained into our fundamental psyche. Above all, stoicism places an emphasis on self-determination, a stance that could be called individualistic or Smithian today. The most important attribute a person can have in their self-determination is, to add, virtue. Virtue is and will continue to be, to the stoic, the greatest good a person can have.

Resources about stoicism are wide and varied and can be found nearly anywhere information is found, namely on the internet. As has been mentioned, some of the most famous Stoic philosophers are Zeno of Citium, Cleanthes, Chrysippus, Diogenes of Babylon, Antipater of Tarsus, Panaetius, Posidonius, Seneca, Musonius Rufus, Epictetus, and Marcus Aurelius. This is of course too long of a list to study all these names in great depth, so it should also be mentioned that the most important of these names are Zeno of Citium, Antipater of Tarsus, Posidonius, Seneca, Epictetus, and Marcus Aurelius. The latter list should be looked into primarily.

It would also be wise to set up certain times at which you can focus on studying these ancient masters and their works. If you stick to scheduling times towards studying these works then you will see more long-term results and you will hold yourself more responsible for studying regularly, which should be done daily.

Quick Start Action Step:

Your first Quick Start Action Step is all about learning more about Stoicism. There are simply too many resources on the internet regarding stoic philosophy to be mentioned here, but any quick Google search of any of the names or concepts listed above would give you lots of material to study further on.

Chapter 2: Ancient Greek and Roman Stoic Philosophy

The term 'stoic' originates from the Greek word for portico or porch: stoa. This is because Zeno of Citium taught most of his lectures on a porch that became famous for these lectures.

The most important feat that the ancient stoic philosophers ever attempted was to provide themselves with a more unified account of the world than other systems had provided. They did this by a wide variety of means, including but not limited to monastic physics, formal logic, and naturalistic ethics. They placed the ethics here as being more important than any other methods listed here, though these other areas have proven to remain of interest to philosophers up to this day.

As far as destructive emotions are concerned, the Stoics preached that it was only self-control and fortitude that could curtail these feelings and faulty thinking patterns. The stoic philosophy of the ancients did not teach that one had to feel only correct emotions, only that one was obligated to control oneself when negative emotions came up. This would, in turn, make people less biased and would, therefore, make them think much more clearly. Once a person would become better able to think clearly, he or she would become much more likely to come closer and closer to the so-called universal reason, or logos, that was always a hallmark of stoic philosophy. The primary objective of practicing stoic philosophy was then to improve on a person's moral and ethical well-being. Here again, virtue consists of a will that is in accordance with nature. As far as interpersonal connections are concerned, stoic philosophy teaches that all of us should avoid jealousy, envy, and anger at all costs. There is also a deep-seated notion of social equality among the ancient Stoic philosophers, some of whom suggested that citizenry should treat their slaves as equals, which was a revolutionary idea at the time.

There are also some bastions of determinism within the teachings of the Stoic creed. While stoicism encourages the study of the natural order of things, this natural order is often left up to something like fate in the minds of many ancient Stoics. In fact, Cleanthes once asserted that wicked men lived like dogs tied to carts, compelled to go wherever they must. The Stoics thought that virtuous people would have to mend their own wills to be in keeping with the natural order of things. This would not necessarily make their fortune any better than it would be otherwise, but it would make them content with their place in life. After this mending had been done to a certain extent the person would then be granted free will for the most part and would continue to live autonomously for the rest of his or her life. On the other hand, the mechanisms of the universe overall would here be left up to a predetermined scheme, another stance that Spinoza would borrow from and develop on.

Stoicism is often labeled by moderns as a philosophy that preaches that we should bear agony and bereavement with fatalistic self-control, which is true to a certain extent, but, as you can already see, there is so much more to the Stoic school of philosophy than just this tiny part of the school's moral philosophy. Stoicism encompasses so much more than it is often given credit for today, which is a shame because if more people knew just how many tenets of stoic philosophy were extolled at one point, they would be much more inclined to study the teachings of the school further.

Stoicism gradually became more popular among the educated elite within the western world of antiquity and was primarily reserved for those who in any age can afford to focus on philosophical study. It was around 300 BC that Zeno of Citium started to first teach his philosophy, which would later grow in popularity to a point at which every successor of Alexander would consider themselves stoic. Stoicism as a school originally started off as something of an offshoot of cynicism, another Greek school of philosophy, this one created by

Antisthenes. From the cynics, the Stoics adopted the ideas that the purpose of life was to live a virtuous life that agrees with nature, and that to gain happiness, people would have to first live a life of rigorous training, in which they would need to act in accordance with nature. The Stoics also preached that a person should live in direct harmony with the universe as a whole, over which no one has any direct control.

Stoicism within its historical context is often classified into three broad categories:
Early stoa, which consists of the founding of the school to Zeno of Antipater.
Middle stoa, which consists of Panaedius and Posidonius.
Later stoa, which consists of Seneca, Musonius Rufus, Epictetus, and Marcus Aurelius.

One of the greatest achievements of stoicism is its advent of propositional logic by Diodorus Cronus. This system differs from any Aristotelian models in that the logic here is not based on terms but is rather based on statements and or propositions. Later, the faculty of deduction would be added to this system of logic to create the definitive system of Stoic logic. All of this can be used in order to ascertain the truth in any given train of thought because here we can focus on the validity of any statements or propositions given to us. This harkens back to the previous point made about adjusting thinking errors and incorrect judgments made regarding certain situations. Stoicism here allows us to analyze the initial propositions given to us or the ones that we give to ourselves.

There are also certain categories within stoic writing that occur frequently and should therefore be defined here. These terms can be found in virtually any works of the great Stoic philosophers: substance, or the primary matter that all things are made out of. Quality, or the way in which matter has been manipulated into forming an object. In stoic physics, this refers to the physical ingredient that a thing is made out of. Somehow disposed, or the particular characteristics that an object has, and somehow disposed in relation to something, or the characteristics that something has in common with something else.

These definitions may seem overly academic or even needless to someone who doesn't have much of a background in philosophy, but if these are applied to everyday life you may be surprised to find just how much utility these terms can provide when it comes to the investigation into the true nature of the world around him or her.

Many modern philosophical minds are in line with the teachings of stoicism in that stoicism teaches us that it is through reason and reason alone that knowledge can be found. Truth in the manner becomes distinguishable from fallacy when reason is applied by the thinker. This is a truism that has been relevant in all ages and will remain so. The Stoics also believed that the sensory organs are constantly being stimulated by external sensory information and that this information then leaves an impression on the imagination (or phantasia). Under this model, it becomes clear that whatever we put into our brains is bound to stay there whether we like it or not, so it would be wise to censor whatever it is that is being inputted into our minds. The age-old adage "you reap what you sow" applies here as it does anywhere.

We are able to distinguish the true from the false as a result of our capacity to judge the impression that we are met with. With more factual judgments we can apprehend truths more readily, but with more subjective ones we have to form only opinions and work our ways hesitantly from there. As opposed to just forming opinions and beliefs, it requires clear and prolonged reasoning to arrive at more clear-cut convictions and more reliable comprehension of the natural order of things. In order to ascertain more true and certain knowledge, by stoic estimations, it is first necessary to verify convictions beyond reasonable doubt using the aid of one's own reasoning as well as the ideas of other people.

The main reason for stoicism being so widely misunderstood by contemporary minds is the fact that many of the terms applied in ancient stoicism take on different meanings today than they originally did. Today the term stoic is often applied to any person who shows or feels little to no emotion. this is due to the fact that stoicism teaches that we can release ourselves from our passions by using nothing but reason. It is not so much the case that stoicism seeks to eliminate emotions altogether, it is more that stoicism encourages the development of inner calm and clear judgment. The most commonly used methods for coming to this clear judgment were and still are logic, concentration, and reflection. these are great tools to use whenever negative emotions present themselves because they allow us to look at situations more objectively.

The stoics borrowed from the cynics the notion that good is inherent within the soul and is manifested through self-control and wisdom. This is a notion that Rousseau would later reiterate. While a person should follow his or her passions in stoic practice, the school also propounds that people should free themselves from such passions. The only difference here is that the ancient Greek translation of the word passion is something similar to anguish or suffering. It is sophistication that is the result of sound and correct judgment, and passion, on the other hand, is always the result of unsound and incorrect judgment.

The idea stoicism is primarily known for in modern times is that through apathy or indifference to suffering one could gain peace of mind. This apathy or indifference could only be obtained through clear judgment in sound reasoning. This concept and its application are still relevant today and holds true through the ages. Here being objective throughout all things can only be done by achieving equanimity of emotions throughout all of life's vicissitudes. While this may seem like a boring or stale mode of being, it does provide a sense of security and stability.

Another concept that is prevalent throughout the works of all the great stoic philosophers is the concept of the logos or the universal reason. Connecting with this reason consists of looking into the natural order of things and using logic to determine the rules by which the universe is held together. This is why the Stoics asserted that to live by virtue and by reason his to follow the logos or be aligned with Nature's will. This also involves recognizing the common reason and the inherent value of every other living creature. Here again is a concept that will more than likely hold true so long as mankind exists.

There are four cardinal virtues in the school of stoicism. These virtues are exalted among all others within this philosophical system:

Wisdom (or Sophia)

Courage (or Andreia)

Justice (or Dikaiosyne)

And Temperance (or Sophrosyne)

It should be clear to you that these four virtues are still just as relevant today as they were at their inception. Like Socratic thinkers, the Stoics held that evil and unhappiness in the world both stemmed from people's ignorance of the natural order of the universe. If, for example, someone happens to be unkind to another, then this disposition derives mainly from that person being out of line or being ignorant of the logos for a universal reason. While notions such as these ones may be considered dogmatic to a few, there is great validity in asserting that people would do much more good if they were to follow the universal reason more often.

Chapter 3: How to be a Stoic in Today's Fast-Paced World

If we are observing stoicism as a philosophy which extols the value in self-control, then it will come as no surprise to us to learn that stoicism may not capture the same footing as other philosophical systems in this age of oversharing. Those who exhibit the same traits that many of the ancient stoic philosophers put forth (such as perceived coldness, aloofness, and or distance) are often singled out and ostracized in today's world. Here the greatest American sin of not being a people person hurts its practitioners in many ways. There is, however, great value to be found in a system such as stoicism, which runs contrary to the passion-fueled nonsense of the time in which we live. While living by stoic principles may not give you many friends in the short term, it will benefit you in the long term, the only stipulation here is that you have to be willing to run against the grain in a world that is being unhinged by generations of freed desire. While the moral relativism of postmodern thought might have some things to teach us, stoicism has just as much, if not more, to offer.

One of the main things that make stoicism appealing and useful today is that it was built for hard times, which is exactly what we are being presented with as a globe. Stoicism as a system was first formed shortly after Alexander's conquest of the Hellenistic world, which was a time of great chaos and warfare. This atmosphere resulted in a philosophical school that offered peace and security to its adherents. While stoicism did not offer the promise of a blissful afterlife like Christianity would later do, it did offer some great guidelines as to how to find happiness reliably within this life.

The philosophy of stoicism asserts that no secure and lasting happiness can be found within this life in things that are able to be manipulated and are temporary. It is only our inner selves that can never leave us, which is exactly what we should focus on the become happier people. Everything else, from all our material possessions to our careers, to even our friends and family members all leave us at one point or another, which is exactly why in order for us to find true happiness we need to be happy with our inner selves, a point that many modern philosophers and psychologists still make to this day.

While it is more than possible that this world will at one point or another take everything away from us, stoicism teaches us that we can still maintain fortitude within our inner worlds and that that will always be enough for us to keep moving on. He again the point that all unhappiness stems from our ignorance of the logos and our inability to fix and maintain our own inner lives.

We are faced with many pains as modern people, just like our ancestors were, and here again, the same stoic concept of treating both painful emotions and rewarding ones with the same level of excitement can be applied to our advantage. Life is not divorceable from suffering, so one method of dealing with this suffering is by accepting it as a natural and necessary part of being. Doing this does not entail making our suffering out to be worse than it truly is, but it does entail accepting what we have been given with a certain amount of self-control.

Another surprising tenet of stoicism is the emphasis it places on universal brotherhood. This makes this philosophy perfectly suited to the intellectual needs of a globalized world. Stoicism, while being born in a time of great patriarchy and intolerance, was the first major philosophy to put forth that all men have things that unite them and that everyone should be treated with the same amount of respect and be given the same rights. This idea may seem like common sense to us today, but in antiquity this was revolutionary.

Another way in which stoicism is just as relevant today as it was at its inception lies within the fact that this philosophy is famously similar to Christianity. Some of the most famous and important ideas that Christianity offers us were not originally created by Christian thinkers, but rather by stoic philosophers, for example, the idea of all humans being brothers fathered by one creator God, mastering and moderating our most basic urges rather than just flatly giving into them, the suggestion that will we invariably fail at some point or another in our lives, and that God is unitary. It was the Stoics, not the Christians, who first came up with all of these ideas before Christianity even existed.

Christianity, with these points being made, is clearly a very stoic religion, and a very conservative one in contrast to many of the other religions which were formed throughout antiquity. As Christianity grew, however, the leaders of the church tried to downplay the influence of the religion within Christian thought, and to some avail, at least publicly, but Christianity remains a fundamentally stoic religion even to this day. If you are inclined to Christian modes of thinking then not only will you more than likely find stoic thought appealing, but you probably already observe lots of the same rules that were originally laid out by the ancient Stoic philosophers.

A trait that stoicism has to offer in all ages is its capacity for leadership. This is especially useful today, where the intellectual climate allows for each and every person to be his or her own God. Stoicism teaches us that in order to control certain events we first have to control ourselves. Further, whatever influences we try to exert on the external world around us are subject to failures and misjudgments, while any influences that we exert on ourselves can succeed 100% of the time. A stoic attitude in a leader protects that leader in the face of failure, and also curtails arrogance in the face of any successes.

Each and every one of us faces uncertainty all of the time. It is leaders, however, that this uncertainty can often take the biggest toll on as far as mental health is concerned. Stoicism does not allow a leader to curtail uncertainty, but it does allow him or her to deal with it gracefully and with a certain degree of maturity.

The Stoics taught that we fail far more often than we succeed. They also taught that being human entails being angry, selfish, and fearful beyond what is necessary. To be human, to the stoic, is to err. This viewpoint may be out of line with the common arrogance and pride of many moderns, which is exactly why many moderns need this type of teaching in their lives. In today's age, if everyone is left up to their own devices, then there will never be any checking anyone's hubris and we will be left with generation after generation of narcissistic pedantry. Stoicism, therefore, has a lot to offer the modern world in the way of avoiding haughtiness.

Quick Start Action Steps

As far as developing a unified approach to stoicism in the modern world is concerned, this can be done much in the same way that it has been done in all past ages.

1. There is one basic tenet which should be kept in mind here that is taught today in many rational emotive behavior therapies: we have the power to create our own emotional destinies. Modern living is beset on all sides by situations which may cause us panic and confusion at times, but there are means to curtail any anxiety that stems from all of these situations. When you are in a state of anxiety, which many moderns increasingly find themselves in frequently regardless of whether or not they have any type of anxiety-related disorders, your amygdala, and your hippocampus act up. These two parts of your limbic system then send out chemical messengers such as adrenaline and glucocorticoids throughout your entire body, while your adrenal glands start to produce cortisol, your body's primary stress hormone.

While messengers such as adrenaline, glucocorticoids, and cortisol can have very positive benefits in the short term as far as basic survival mechanisms are concerned, prolonged excess of any of these messengers can have detrimental impacts on the brain and of the body, including high blood pressure and even permanent brain damage. This is due to two causes, one is that the body's entire nervous and endocrine systems are thrown out of balance by excesses or poverties of certain chemical messengers such as neurotransmitters and hormones, and the second is that when an excess of a certain messenger is being produced, available vitamins and nutrients are being spent in excess to produce that specific chemical messenger, making them unavailable for the production of any other chemical messengers.

2. One step to take in your everyday life that could be deduced from all of this information is that you can manipulate your body by the

things that you ingest. If, for example, you expose yourself to lots of plastic products and exhaust fumes while still eating lots of highly processed foods, then you are bound to have higher levels of estrogen in your system, making your entire body less healthy than it would otherwise be. If you want to have an overall healthier body then obtaining this is going to start with what you put into your body. Once these more balanced levels of the chemical messengers within your nervous and endocrine systems have been established your brain and mind will then follow suit and become healthier themselves.

3. Stoicism teaches us to treat the anxiety-inducing thoughts and situations with the same equanimity that we treat everything else in our lives. This is not to imply that we have to pretend to be apathetic towards these thoughts and situations, but we should be mature in realizing that these are passing issues that will not end our world entirely. Staying cool-headed throughout these periods of chaos and

confusion will always be rewarded by greater clarity of mind and greater wisdom eventually.

4. The next tool that more or less all modern people need to use is mindfulness training. This training requires of us that we create more rational, stable, and non-debilitating emotional systems for ourselves that will leave us acting more stable and alert in times of great crisis in our lives. Everyone is subjected to floods of some type or another within the course of their lives, so it is not the people who go without these floods who get ahead, because those people simply do not exist, but it is rather those of us who know how to deal with these happenings in an appropriate manner who do.

Mindfulness is always best achieved when it is practiced each and every day. In order to correct your thinking pattern and faulty emotions effectively and to keep them corrected it is necessary to keep meditating and keep reiterating the positive points that you make to yourself on a daily basis. More often than not doing this requires taking the time to schedule out certain times within your days towards practicing these concepts. This will wind up being a long-term investment that will at first not show any reward but will later start to benefit you immensely in whatever it is that you are trying to accomplish. By this, it is meant that there is a plateau of latent potential that is met when you first start to develop a habit, which in this case would be mindfulness training, in which there are no immediate rewards that make themselves clear to you. It is only after this stage of putting lots of time into the formation of the habit and not getting any immediate reward that the participant starts to see some rewards throughout a short period of time known as the phase transition.

Once this phase transition has been passed through, there is little to no room for improvement, but there still remains the necessity of maintaining the habit. This is when we become capable of maintaining our clarity of mind throughout times of great crisis. While this may seem like a simple thing to do when everything is going well, hard times always take lots of preparation to get through. And all of this is what it is meant when it is said that we have the power to create our emotional destinies.

Philosophical education is surprisingly hard to come by in modern times. It is disappointing that philosophy often receives the reputation of a practice that is more theoretical than practical and that it is more often practiced by academics who do not consider its real-world applications so much as they busy themselves with impressing their colleagues.

While the stoic philosophy might justifiably be considered a dense one with lots of seemingly pedantic technicalities about it, it still has a lot to offer us in our everyday lives, so long as it is continually practiced. There is here, as there is anywhere, a fine distinction between extolling certain philosophical virtues and actually going about living by them. In order to truly live by the stoic creed, it is necessary to not only read the works of the great Stoic philosophers but also to take steps actively to apply their teachings to our everyday lives in order to get genuine benefits from what they say and to improve on our common thinking patterns.

Another problem that many moderns face is the problem of media oversaturation. While there is nothing within the works of any of the ancient stoics relating to this problem, it is mindfulness training that will ultimately be of the greatest benefit to us in terms of curtailing any of the negative effects of this saturation. Whether we notice it or not, all of the media that we are constantly consuming every day is having massive impacts on us in terms of things like attention span and memory. Stoic meditation can give us an opportunity to escape from all of this excess information and to detach from the world within our phones, forcing us to reconnect with whatever is inside of ourselves and whatever we find immediately in the world around us.

Chapter 4: Applying the Stoic Teachings – Marcus Aurelius

Marcus Aurelius was and continues to be arguably the most important stoic philosopher of antiquity. In addition to his philosophical work, he was also a Roman emperor for a time. From an early age, he was given one of the greatest educations that could have been asked for in antiquity, being in constant contact with some of the most influential orators and intellectuals at that time. His son would later, as could be expected, come to loathe learning and all of the figures that he himself would come into contact with within the academic world. He much preferred the hardening qualities of military life as opposed to the softening qualities of intellectual life.

To give some historical context regarding this figure, throughout Marcus Aurelius' reign as emperor the Roman Empire defeated the Parthian Empire and won the Marcomannic wars in the west against the Marcomanni, the Sarmatians, and the Quadi. The persecution of Christians, however, was shown to increase during Aurelius' reign.

Marcus Aurelius was originally educated within the confines of the contemporary aristocratic trends of the day. He was trained in philosophy and oration by private teachers, most of whom followed Socratic and platonic modes of thought rather than stoic ones. Some of them even went so far as to criticize stoicism publicly. It was not until later on in his life that Aurelius would be drawn over to stoicism once and for all.

Aurelius' most famous and widely read contribution to stoic thought is his Meditations. This is a series of writings containing some of Aurelius' most important pieces of life advice that were the favorite of figures from Frederick the Great and John Stuart Mill to Goethe and Bill Clinton. This work is widely held as one of the most important philosophical works in history. The title of this series literally translates to "Things to oneself."

The central theme of this ambitious work is that one should always strive to analyze his or her own judgments regarding him or herself and others, and in doing this Aurelius propounds that one can find a more cosmic perspective on the reality of the nature of things. Here he encourages stripping away any superfluous presuppositions in order to find clearer judgment and more rational thinking, allowing a person to step outside of him or herself in order to ascertain the truth of things from a higher plane. Within this text, Aurelius also puts lots of value in the pursuit of good character traits, rather than just the open assertions of one's own intrinsic goodness.

Here Aurelius also asserts the value of divorcing oneself from any affections and claims that in doing so a person will save his or herself from lots of future hardship brought on by the material world. Here he goes on to assert that the only way in which a person can be harmed in life is to let his or her emotions overpower his or her betters' faculties. Here again, a notion of logos or universal reason permeates all things and should always be followed in order to develop any clearer reasoning and or any sounder judgments. Here we would also be wise in doing away with any preconceived notions of good or bad. Things that are effectually out of our control are here considered by Aurelius as being neither good nor bad.

Marcus Aurelius also extols the value of bearing misfortune with self-control in his meditations. Here he teaches us that rather than complaining about certain misfortunes we should be grateful to still be alive after said misfortunes. Very few people live by this creed, although nearly everyone, tends to pride themselves on being able to handle tragedy well. Related to this point, Aurelius also warns against dwelling on the past and questioning why we are always met with so much tragedy. He is a progressive in that he continually looks forward to the future, no matter whatever may happen in it.

The meditations also take on something of a deterministic patina. Here Aurelius asserts that all actions and all happenings were set in stone at the beginning of time and that therefore there is no free will, which runs contrary to all of the points made on personal development and conduct, but these points remain valid nevertheless.

Marcus Aurelius, being the most famous and influential stoic philosopher of antiquity, created a philosophy which people have come to know stoicism in its most quintessential form in terms of. All of the most important and famous tenets of stoic philosophy met their culmination in Marcus Aurelius, so reading his works remains one of the most important parts of understanding the system as a whole.

While the concepts listed here may seem more fit for theoretical academia than actual everyday life, there still remain lots of areas in which the teachings of Marcus Aurelius remain relevant today. As is the case in nearly every major historical figure, there are innumerable lessons to be learned from the life of this man which would be wise in applying to his or her everyday life.

Seeing as how this figure doubled as a political figure in addition to being a philosopher, we can learn not only a lot about stoic philosophy from him, but we can also learn a lot about the common themes among all of the most powerful figures in world history that were in place within his character. Just as the Bible taught all those who read it by going over what all of the kings of Israel had in common throughout antiquity, here to history can teach us what holds to be most useful in leaders and in everyday people throughout all ages.

His early education, along with his subsequent reaction to said education, shows us one trend, in particular, that of the inception of the hero's journey (in a Jungian sense) and the abandonment of many of the educational structures and maxims that were originally instilled within the hero throughout his youth. No personage of any great importance and or influence has ever simply stuck to doing the same things that his or her predecessors have done in the past. If no adaptations are ever made to a belief of a thought system then that thought system is bound to implode in on itself just as soon as any information comes along that contradicts any of the maxims set forth by that system. There is no sense in applying the same concepts throughout different periods of time in which those concepts prove to be irrelevant, but there are certain concepts that hold true in any given age. The life of Marcus Aurelius and his detachment from the earlier models of thought that he grew up learning extols this fact famously.

His meditations are full to the brim with great advice suitable for practical use within everyday life. The central theme of this work is something like constantly analyzing one's own inner thoughts in order to ascertain better and clearer judgment. The ways in which this concept can be practically applied in everyday life are so multifarious that it is hard to imagine. Within any given problem that we are presented with, there is a great opportunity to apply this concept. It should be noted here that this has to be done throughout a prolonged period of time though. Many often make the mistake of attempting to adjust their faulty attitudes and thinking patterns just once and then determining that they are effectually cured of erroneous thought for life. The path towards intellectual success is a meandering one though, and it requires constant pushing of one's own boundaries to get anywhere intellectually.

This point is closely related to another one made about any harm being done to a person being the result of that person not reading to his or her greater faculties, but instead letting his or her emotions get the better of the person.

This remains as important of a point today as it was when the Meditations were originally written, arguably more important. To live in modernity is to have what is more or less too much freedom as far as following our passions is concerned. Many people take an Orwellian view on the downfall of modern people, that is to say that they think that it is hardships of some sorts that bring us down, but the Stoics preached more of what we could call a Huxleyan view today in that they believed that more people are brought down by getting all that they want. When you have nothing but temporary passions motivating your behavior, you will get nothing but the fulfillment of those temporary passions in return. It is like living the life of a hamster on one of their wheels, it is getting nowhere while still putting forth maximal effort.

There is yet another axiom that Marcus Aurelius sets forth that states that we should always focus on bearing the tragedies of life with a certain amount of self-control. This is not a trait that is common among very many people today, but those of us who do focus on developing this trait are rewarded greatly for doing so. Rather than jumping to conclusions and flying off the handle in situations in which we are put at a disadvantage, stoicism teaches us to remain level-headed in periods of great chaos.

Quick Start Action Steps

In order to apply Marcus Aurelius' principles to one's everyday life one must:

1. Commit to constantly adjusting one's viewpoints regarding problems:

> This one is helpful regarding combating negative emotions, whatever they might be. Here Marcus Aurelius asserts to us that all of our suffering is just a product of faulty perceptions that we carry out on the things that we come into contact with. In order to free ourselves from

these faulty perceptions, it is necessary to ask ourselves why we feel the ways that we do and what thinking patterns would be more rational than the ones that we currently hold.

Let's say you're having issues with a family member for example. The Stoics, and later the behaviorists, would tell you in this case that you should focus on stripping away any and all presuppositions regarding this family member that you may hold. This allows the family member to be free of any wrongdoings in the past from your own estimation. Rather than using categorical thinking to put this family member in some type of camp, you are allowing him or her to grow, and you are also allowing yourself to notice things about this person that you may have not seen before. As far as whether or not his or her behaviors change, only the future can tell, but in the present, it is important not to behold others with too much judgment.

2. Focus more on one's actual actions rather than just his or her perceptions or moral assertions:

> Jung, as well as, nearly all other modern thinkers, thought that it was much harder to live by one's principles than to extol them and that the Judeo-Christian notion of the judge and the redeemer usually let people get away with a bit too much. This is a notion that many modern people, especially those whose values are in line with the tenets of postmodern philosophy, find too constricting to live by. People love their freedoms, which is a trait that is not being curtailed by the overwhelming strength of modern states but is rather being exalted by it. There still remains, however, great value in those who truly live by their own values. In an age of

flakiness and noncommittal behaviors, the age-old adage "thoughts speak louder than words" is more important to reiterate than ever.

3. Suffering should be met with some degree of self-control:

> Adults often respond to life's vicissitudes much in the same ways that they did as children, that is to say, they become victims of the random designs of some creator whose inner workings they will never truly understand. Stoicism teaches us that this is not a noble stance to take in the face of hardship and that suffering should be met with the same energy that good fortune is met with.
>
> While it is always important never to trivialize any of the things that hurt yourself or others, stoicism teaches us that these happenings do not define us as victims and that we should keep our

wits about us when going through hard times. A corollary of this point is that it is from the hard things in life that we encounter that we always learn the greatest lessons. This corollary was extolled by modern Yale based composer David Lang in his "Sweet Air" for chamber orchestra. It is suffering, as Hobbes thought, that is the cause of all the greatest products of mankind.

4. Reject the offerings of the material world:

Aurelius also reminds us that material goods do not lead to any greater happiness, a point that needs to be made continually to all those who live in the modern consumer-based world. Modern social science backs this assertion up with its findings of hedonistic treadmills being developed among people above a certain wealth percentile on which additional income does not correlate with greater happiness or general well-being.

Chapter 5: Applying the Stoic Teachings – Epictetus

Epictetus was born in Phrygia in A.D. 55 and spent his childhood working as a slave to one of Emperor Nero's secretaries. He would develop a passion for philosophy early in his life and was eventually allowed by his master to study with the Stoic Musonius Rufus. He then became crippled, some say by his master's doing. Epictetus is unique within his time both in that he was able to gain his freedom and that he was able to go on to become a notable philosopher.

He originally taught philosophy in Rome until around 93 A.D. when Emperor Domitian banished all philosophers from the city. From that point, he traveled to Nicopolis, where he would then start his own school of philosophy. Epictetus was noted as a gifted orator as well, one who could imbue all of the passions within his reader that he wanted to. On the whole, he was well liked and even Emperor Hadrian was supplicant in his company.

As far as his lifestyle is concerned, he lived alone for the most part and very modestly, with little to no personal possessions to weigh him down. It wasn't until his old age that he finally started living with a woman, an arrangement that was made only to raise the child of a friend more effectively who would have been otherwise left to die. From this point he would live out the remainder of his long life and eventually die in 135 A.D.

      The main work that Epictetus is known for is the Discourses, although it was only one of his pupils who wrote this work, transcribing it from discourses that he had heard. Within these discourses, only four of which still remain, Epictetus asserts that self-knowledge is the foundation of all philosophy. It would therefore follow that we need to first admit our gullibility and ignorance before gaining any additional knowledge. While logic might provide us with improved reasoning and clarity of judgment, it is still subordinate to our immediate practical needs, at least as Epictetus propounds. Once Epictetus had established the foundation of all philosophy, he then asserted that the first rule of philosophy was that its followers need to follow the doctrines that they decide to, in other words, that they should genuinely live by the philosophical principles that they themselves subscribe to, which is an idea that Marcus Aurelius later served as a scion to. The second rule consisting of why people should not lie, and the third putting forth and examining the reasons why people should not lie.

There is also a distinction made between things within our power (or prophereitic things), and things that are not within our power (or aprophereitic things) made at the beginning of the discourse. Within the realm of things within our power, Epictetus includes things such as aversions, desires, impulses, and opinions. There are also mentioned many things that are not within our power within this discourse, such as power, glory, possessions, and bodies. When we delude ourselves as to what is within our power and what is without it, we are then confronted with slavery of the soul, the greatest troubles, errors, and misfortunes that we are ever met with. Here Epictetus reminds us that we ultimately have no power over anything external within our lives and that therefore it is the goodness in our own inner lives that we should focus on primarily in order to find any lasting happiness.

Next Epictetus determines that the difference between good and evil is made within us by our own free choice. Here he differs from Aurelius' more deterministic system in asserting that we ultimately have some sort of free will, though it is still kept that this will cannot be exerted over out external reality in any reliable manner. Our reason then determines our courses of action based on what is making sensory impressions on us at any given point in time.

This viewpoint involving things being out of our control also provides us with means of detaching ourselves peacefully from the things that we cannot exert any influence over. Something ceases to be ours once we accept that we have no power over it, which is freeing to us because we no longer have to worry about its happenings. It is similar to the point Rousseau made regarding love: when we love something, we in turn become possessive of it, and this opens the door to jealousy to enter our hearts. Likewise, when we think that we can control anything outside of us we are much more upset when something comes along that proves this presupposition to be a false one. Such an important part of stoic wisdom is the ability to accept our own ignorance as well as your inability to influence the things outside of you.

The practical implications of Epictetus' writings are as numerous as their theoretical implications. We should here start with the concept of self-knowledge. To find an area of life in which self-knowledge is not important to obtain is an impossible task to achieve. It could even be argued that there is no knowledge besides self-knowledge, because all forms of knowledge stem from the mind, and are therefore never divorced from the workings of the mind.

In order to obtain greater self-knowledge, it is necessary to analyze the thinking patterns that we find ourselves living by every day. Often these patterns are repeated rather consistently (unless we are taking a more behavioristic stance which would assert that these patterns do not exist in the first place), so any faulty thinking patterns that are repeated throughout our considerations of multiple things are going to continue to inhibit our growth until we address them effectively. These thinking patterns are often labeled schema by modern psychotherapists, which are often instilled into our minds at early ages and usually take years to reverse the negative effects of, if they are ever reversed at all.

The emphasis that Epictetus places on logic is obviously very practically applicable to everyday life. Bettering one's logical resources can be achieved through a number of means including laying one's own premises out clearly, providing evidence that supports one's own premises, and drawing clearly delineated connections to conclusions of trains of thought. Epictetus does also, however, also emphasize the importance of more immediately practical tasks over the more esoteric logical structures.

Epictetus also extols the value of telling the truth and nothing but the truth. Telling the truth is not only the only morally acceptable mode of communication, but it also happens to be the most effective mode of being possible. You never have to backtrack on what you say when you never lie, you also do not have to worry as much about how you are presenting yourself. While the total avoidance of lying may seem like a fairly straightforward and simple concept to most, living by this tenet often proves harder to lots of people than it should rightly be, especially to those of us who may happen to live around dishonest company.

Next, we are told that we need to observe the distinction made between things that are within our power and things that are not. The practical implications of this piece of advice are infinitesimal. This could be especially helpful for many modern people to keep in mind regarding workplace stress, one of the most destructive health concerns throughout the modern world. If you look towards things at work (or anywhere else, for that matter) that you have no control over as being stressors, then you are expending lots of needless energy on things that you cannot change whatsoever. There is one anecdote that can be brought to mind on this subject of Warren Buffett once telling one of his pupils to make a list of his 25 top priorities. Once this list had been made Buffett told the pupil to keep only the five things at the top of the list and disregard everything else. This goes to show that it is only the things that we love to do the most and the things that we cannot stand to do but are still necessary that we should focus most of our time on. It is the little things that we only somewhat enjoy and take up side projects that usually waste the largest amount of our time and should therefore be culled out of our schedules wherever possible.

This idea of accepting that we have no real control over external forces is closely related to Epictetus' point made on accepting our own ignorance and fallibility. If we are not willing to accept that we are limited in what we can do and can think then we will never make any notable progress towards gaining more knowledge of the world around us and or towards clearing up our personal judgments in relation to external things.

Finally, we would also do well to detach ourselves from all of the material goods that we have, at least insofar as we are not keeping things that are not necessary for us to have in the first place. This can and should be done easily by being honest with oneself regarding what one needs vs. what one wants, the two are typically much out of line with one another. Ridding yourself of any superfluous possessions will make you feel much more natural and self-reliant. It is a step towards living more simplistically that not nearly enough people of today ever have the courage to take.

Here we should go over more clearly how to apply some of Epictetus' concepts to issues that people are commonly faced with in everyday life. You may find here that while these concepts were propounded thousands of years ago and while they have primarily theoretical applications, they can still be found to have very much utility in everyday living, even in modern life.

Quick Start Action Steps

1. Gain and foster self-knowledge

Many people today make the mistake of filling up their own inner lives needlessly with the opinions of others. This makes it hard to distinguish our own self-concepts from the thoughts of others regarding us. In this age of more or less constant interconnection with the world brought on by our devices, it becomes increasingly difficult to tune all who we know out and to focus only on our own innermost thoughts and feelings. Mindfulness training of some sort usually proves to be of very much use when trying to develop one's self-knowledge. So many people get so absorbed in taking in more or less constant information from their devices that they rarely, if ever, take the opportunity to simply disconnect for some amount of time in order to clear their heads and set their minds back to a natural starting point.

Another thing to consider regarding self-knowledge is the formation of thinking patterns. From a psychological perspective, the manipulation of these patterns can be performed most reliably by daily affirmations. These should be repeated to oneself on a daily basis and should eventually lead to one giving off certain different impressions to others. This will, in turn, cause one to be perceived differently by those who he or she knows, usually creating a self-systemic loop of greater external respect found followed by greater self-respect found and so on and so forth. If memory is to be considered the byproduct of repetition, then affirmations of some sort would, in turn, be the best ways in which to adjust one's own thinking patterns and to lock those adjustments into one's long-term memory. Writing one's own thoughts down or expressing them audibly also helps here. It is very often that people are set back by thoughts that they themselves cannot keep any great track of. Giving oneself some sort of tangible representation of these thoughts, whether it be in writing or a recording of some type, gives one something to observe objectively and clearly, and to adjust wherever one finds fault in these thinking patterns.

2. Bettering logical resources

Betting our logic is our next step towards living more carefully by Epictetus' teachings. There are innumerable ways in which to this, all of which should be carried out throughout extended periods of time. Here we need to focus primarily on laying out clearly delineated premises for ourselves. Again, writing can prove to be extremely useful here. We cannot gain accurate descriptions of the premises that we are propounding to ourselves without some degree of effort, which should usually involve writing of some sort, to better organize our thoughts. Here the stoic idea of detaching yourself from your presuppositions in relation to the matter at hand proves to be just as beneficial as it always is.

3. Tell only the truth

It is never the gigantic lies that eventually lead to a person's downfall, instead, it is always the culmination of many little white lies that build up over time to destroy a person's reputation, along with the relationships of that person. It is these lies, therefore, that we would always be wiser in keeping track of. These lies could be called microhabits, which may not seem to have great impacts on our lives in the short term, but there is a compounding interest that is taken up in these habits which eventually leads us to be beset with greater harm in the long term.

One of the worst things about all of the smaller lies that people tell is that people often do not even notice that they tell these lies, and therefore are eventually not even able to distinguish these lies from truths of any sort. And when a person cannot even tell just how truthful he or she is being with another person, it is usually a good indication that that person is not very honest within his or her inner life, which is where many people's greatest problems stem from.

4. Realize the distinction between what is in one's control and what is not

When this distinction is never made people start to run into greater problems than are necessary, usually by erring on the side of rubbing their noses into places that they have no business in. We can always better ascertain what we have control over by analyzing our actual places in the world. It is never, after all, advisable for a plumber to take up an emperor's work in a day, or vice versa.

Chapter 6: Applying the Stoic Teachings – Seneca

Seneca (or, more specifically, Seneca the younger) was born in Cordova in the Roman province of Hispania. His father, Seneca the elder, was a Roman knight in addition to being a teacher and rhetor. There is controversy over his birth year, which has been estimated between 8 and 1 BC. He then became a Roman resident in 5 A.D.; his father was a regular resident of the city of Rome and taught the usual subjects of rhetoric, grammar, and literature within the city.

Seneca the younger was given one of the best educations that the world had to offer at the time, being taught philosophy by the stoic Attalus, Sotion, and Papirius Fabianus. The latter two of this group were actually members of the School of Sextii, which combined the teachings of stoicism with those of Pythagoreanism. And of these two it was Sotion who convinced Seneca to take up practicing vegetarianism, a practice that Seneca the elder would eventually advise against, associating the diet with those of foreigners. Seneca the younger was plagued by breathing problems throughout the course of his life, more than likely asthma was the most severe among these, though he also contracted tuberculosis around his mid-twenties. He was then sent to live with his Aunt in Egypt, who nursed him through about a decade of ill health. This was a seminal move because it was only through his aunt's influence that Seneca became able to find a seat in the Roman senate.

The early years of Seneca's senatorship were met with great success and much admiration for his abilities in oration. His orations were met with so much praise, in fact, that Caligula soon became jealous of this success and had it ordered that he commit suicide. It was only due to the fact that Caligula was told that Seneca was about to die anyway that he avoided this punishment. It should come as no surprise for us to then learn that in his writings Seneca has next to nothing good to say of Caligula and rather asserts that he is a monster.

In 41 A.D. Claudius became emperor of Rome and Seneca was accused of adultery. He was then sentenced to death by the Senate, a sentence which Claudius eventually commuted to exile. He would then spend the next eight years of his life residing on the island of Corsica. It was within this period of exile that Seneca wrote two of his most famous early works, the Consolidations. In the first of these consolidations, Seneca comforts his mother for here having a son that has been sentenced to exile. He also mentions the death of his only son within this work. In the later consolidation, the Consolidation to Polybius, Seneca is comforting Polybius for the death of his brother. He also mentions that he hopes to be recalled from exile in this work. It was not until 49 A.D., however, that Seneca was returned to Rome and given a praetorship by the Senate.

In 54 A.D. Seneca was appointed an advisorship to emperor Nero, which in turn gave his a suffect consulship. During this consulship, Seneca promised to restore lots of the authority lost by the Senate in the years leading up to his new position. He then wrote his famous essay On Clemency after Nero's murder of Britannicus. While this essay may flatter Nero at times, it is still meant to extol the archetypal path of virtue for a stoic emperor. Seneca would later lose all of his influence over emperor Nero, and would then even agree to his murdering of Agrippa.

In 58 A.D., Senator Publius Rufus started to make a series of public attacks on Seneca. Among the problems listed within these attacks was Seneca's charging high interests on loans taken out within Italy and the provinces, and making a substantial fortune for himself in the process. There were also attacks laid out by other senators, including an accusation that Seneca had slept with Agrippa. This accusation of sexual corruption was originally made by Sulius, who Seneca proclaimed was not an impartial judge in the matter, but instead was in line with the affections of Claudius. Seneca then brought on his own series of convictions against Sulius, who then had his estate confiscated and was exiled promptly.

Seneca's ultimate undoing came in his participation in the Pisonian conspiracy, a plot to kill Nero that was uncovered before it could be carried out. Nero would order Seneca to kill himself after his involvement had been convicted, which he would do by severing several of his veins.

    Seneca the younger's philosophical works focus primarily on the subject of ethics, with the exception of his Naturales Quaestiones, which instead focuses on happenings of the natural world. Throughout Seneca's life stoicism was very popular among upper-class Romans due to the fact that it was seen as the guiding moral framework by which a person could meet political relevance. Seneca was originally given a reputation of a more eclectic philosopher among historiographers, but posterity later remembers him as an orthodox stoic and then as a free thinker by the standards of his time. In the way of his influences, we remember that he frequently cited the works of many earlier Stoics such as Cleanthes, Zeno, Chrysippus. Another profoundly influential philosopher for Seneca was Posidonius, with whom Seneca shared an interest in natural phenomena of all sorts. Epicurus is one more ancient philosopher quotes frequently in Seneca's works.

This interest in the works of Epicurus is wholly limited to the ethical maxims put forth by that philosopher. The works of Plato and other platonic philosophers is the theoretical basis of Seneca's metaphysics. His ethical teachings still remain firmly rooted in stoic traditions, though in Seneca these traditions are expressed with less technical verbiage and are made to be much more accessible.

In addition to ethical theory, most of these works provide sound practical advice, two topics that, while Seneca asserts are distinct from one another, are very much interdependent with one another.

Seneca believes, like many other Stoics, that the universe is governed by some sort of rational providence- an idea that Christianity would later adopt as its own. The only problem with this viewpoint is that it somehow has to be reconciled with adversity, which is precisely what philosophers and thinkers have tried to do ever since. While this problem never solves itself within Seneca's works, he still asserts to us that it is philosophy that is the antidote to all of the suffering involved in living. And in order to minimize suffering, Seneca thought, we must first do away with all of the more destructive passions of grief, anger, etc. This is a viewpoint that is widely contradicted today, as many people often mistake rumination for sorting through their own problems effectively and conclusively. Like other Stoics, he encourages moderating passions according to reason and also extols the virtues in leading an active and contemplative life while also confronting and accepting one's own death.

In his De Vita Beata (or "On the happy life") Seneca, like Marcus Aurelius, argues that nature and reason (logos) are one in the same, and that to achieve lasting happiness one needs to follow this logos by living in accordance with nature at large. It would not be in line with common sense then to diverge from nature's path set aside for us rather than following it. He does, however, meet conformity with a certain degree of scorn, claiming famously that it is always the most well-beaten paths that prove to be the most deceptive. As far as freedom is concerned, Seneca considers the following of God's path or the path of nature to be the key to true freedom. Since people are often inclined to trust others' advice at face value and to simply follow whatever the majority is doing mistakes that occur due to one person's faults of judgment are promptly passed down through many others and eventually cause widespread mistakes being made throughout a larger group of people.

There are many things that these axioms have to offer us in the way of everyday practical advice. Let's start with a discussion of the first axiom here: Follow logos and the will of nature in order to find true happiness. This one is particularly difficult to follow for modern people who are never exposed to nature or who never set enough of their own time aside for introspection of any sort. This is, in fact, an axiom that is so seldom practiced today that many would confuse this practice with superstition. In order to follow this axiom though it would be necessary to devote more time to asking oneself what it is exactly that is wanted and how to obtain it in any given situation. This requires more time and self-knowledge than most people have or are willing to put in, but those who do take a break from their constant flows of information to introspect will always be met with great rewards.

Another axiom pointed out within this work that many modern people would be averse to is the practice of following God or nature's path rather than trying to diverge from it. This is not to say that the stoic needs to follow what any of his or her peers are doing, only what is set before him or her by something greater than him or herself.

The works of Seneca offer us lots of sound and practical advice concerning ethics that are just as relevant today as they were in antiquity. To narrow all of these great points brought up by this thinker, we will now delve into some of the more specific axioms that Seneca propounds.

- Follow logos and live in accordance with the will of nature

This presupposition does not assume that logos will always provide a person with whatever it is that he or she immediately asks for or even expects because, after all, even clear and rational choices can lead us to outcomes that do not work in our favor. It does, however, argue that fate drags the willing and the unwilling along with it indifferently, so it is likely not that we will be rewarded for following our fates with self-control, but that this self-control will make the vicissitudes of life all the more bearable and that we will get out of whatever tribulations we are faced with, with something of our character still intact. This is an important skill to practice because whether or not we practice it, we will always be met with tragedy and suffering, so it proves all the better to "take up our crosses" as Christian thinkers would usually say.

The best way to better follow logos is to, for the most part, follow one's own intuition (but only insofar as one is adjusting any faulty thinking patterns while doing so). It is common for all of us, at least at one point or another, to feel as though we are being told something important by something that is greater than us. It is in these moments that the greatest thoughts that we ever think are created and that the solutions to our problems can become apparent at once to us. If this is done regularly, then not only will we solve our problems, but we will also become great solvers of our own problems, which always has much more utility, at least by the estimates of very many contemporary psychologists. One important theme to be noted here is that of the adage "give a man a fish and he will eat for a day, teach a man to fish and he will eat for a lifetime."

- Avoiding conforming to paradigms that no one is truly certain of

So much of what we do on a daily basis and in all facets of waking life is done solely for the reason that everyone else around us is doing the same. While there usually is a certain degree of validity in upholding the status quo whatever we do not know enough to contradict it, it would be naive to assume that all of the practices put in place by our predecessors and practiced by our peers are always the right things for us to do ourselves. This is a viewpoint that not enough people today take towards a lot of issues, labor especially.

In order to avoid conforming to procedures that we are averse to, we always first have to analyze well the constituent components of the procedure in question. Here Descartes reminds us in his Method for conducting the reason that we should focus on 1. Accepting nothing as true that we do not know for certain to be so, 2. To divide issues that we face into smaller parts, 3. To order these individual components by their difficulties and work our way from easiest to hardest, and 4. To make enumerations so complete and conclusions so clear that we are certain we have left nothing out of consideration.

Here it becomes necessary to replace the old, faulty practice with some sort of new, useful one. If, after all, we do not replace the practice with another that works better, then we will meet a practical abyss which will more than likely be filled by some other practice with the same or less practical value as the original.

- Prefer wealth, but do not be a subordinate to it

While excess wealth may bring temporary happiness, it is ultimately virtue that leads to long-term happiness. This is why Seneca tells us that we should not invest too much of our time acquiring things that we do not need. The consumer-based cultures of today preach an entirely different dogma which needs to be counteracted at every step with the teachings of Seneca. Wealth (in moderation) is not a good or an evil in Seneca's works, which is why it should get about as much attention as does any other neutrality that we are met with. Here again, stoicism preaches absolute indifference towards all of life's trivialities.

Quick Start Action Step:

For your quick start action step, pick one of the points mentioned in the previous section and apply it on an area in your life to bring self-improvement.

Chapter 7: How to Deal with Negative Emotions

Negativity is often more or less impossible to ignore, especially when one finds his or herself in excessively negative company or in negative living situations. This point does not imply that negativity is something to always be ignored, however. Here we do not have the questions of whether or not we will experience negative thoughts and feelings or how to ignore these, but we instead have the question of what to do with these thoughts and how to use them to our advantage.

Negativity, as well as positivity, in most situations, is more a product of the mind than anything else. It is usually a product of our own outlooks more so than any particulars of the situation at hand. There are, however, some negative situations that are detrimental to us regardless of how we look at them, though our perceptions of them are by no means arbitrary. It is from these situations, however, that some of life's greatest rewards are brought to us. When experiencing hard things stoicism teaches us to use our faculty of reason to our advantage so that we can better detach from any negatives of the situation and look at what is happening more objectively. This additional objectivity is accompanied by a greater perspective on matters, which will, in turn, lead to different (and better) decision making on the reasoner's part.

One of the greatest tenets that stoic philosophy offers in the way of improving on dealing with negative emotions is the assertion that we should not try to control the things that are not rightfully in our power. This acceptance is not a passive one, however, it only implies that we should be realistic with ourselves regarding what we can actually do to influence the world around us. To try to overstep our boundaries is a common mistake that all too many people make and that leads to so much needless hardship brought on by vanity.

The main set of negative emotions that plague most people consists of depression, envy, anxiety, vanity, and anger. The two main strategies that we can use in order to curtail these bothersome emotions are becoming an observer and remaining aware of these emotions. These two points, for the most part, harken back to the previous point made about detaching from negative emotions and looking objectively into their cause and solutions.

Envy

It would now be wise to go over how to better deal with all of these emotions individually. Here we will start off with envy. Envy is one of the most destructive emotions that we can face due to the fact that it can lead to resentment and bitterness, distress and discontent, causes us to do things that we would usually never do otherwise, and it can even lead to depression.

The next time that this emotion is felt by the reader, he or she should consider a number of propositions which will help curtail the negative thinking patterns associated with this detrimental emotion. The first of these propositions, or better - strategies, is to shift your focus towards all of the good things that you have going on in your own life. One of or maybe the most common sources of envy that people have for others is their own inability to see all of the things that they have to be grateful for in their own lives. Once we open ourselves up to seeing all of the great things that we have in reality, we are finally reminded that our own lives are too valuable to be lived by any others.

It should also be noted that comparing our own lives to those of others never works in our favor because we are always comparing the worst in ourselves to the best that we assume in others. We would do well to keep in mind here that no one has it all and that we are all faced with a similar amount of adversity, for the most part.

If we understand ourselves to be people with proclivities towards envy, then we should avoid spending time around those who only value the wrong things in life. Peer pressure is a very real force. If, for instance, we spend all of our time around competitive pianists, then we are going to be much more likely to think competitively on the piano, which is not a bad thing. It is people with adverse value systems then, who should be avoided as much as possible. If we find ourselves forced to be around such people, then it becomes necessary to double down on our own values and to respect our own way of living as much, if not more, than the ways of our company.

The next proposition is the other side of the previous one. It is always better to spend more time around grateful people. This will make it so much easier to be grateful ourselves because the attitude will be natural among our company. Here again, peer pressure can have a great impact on our own character, only in this case, the impact is a positive one.

One final proposition to avoid envy is that we should keep in mind that our media is constantly trying to make us more envious so we would be wise to avoid advertisements wherever possible. Avoiding these will not only make us less envious but will also make us less desirous.

Depression

Depression is one disorder that can be treated effectively if it is taken up actively, but the hard part of doing so is often the initial activity being taken up, as depression can drain willpower and energy in a way that few if any, other disorders can. In fact, simply thinking about the steps that one should take in order to overcome his or her depression can seem overwhelming to a depressive. These initial steps in gaining activity and doing something with one's life are always the hardest but are also the most important. Once momentum has been established in any given activity, however, it becomes much easier to continue performing the task at hand. Once the plateau of latent potential in which lots of investment is being made but no results are shown has been passed by a phase transition in which the participant reaps the reward of his or her efforts is gone under. This is where exponential growth along with other great rewards can be found. This concept applies to any type of habit formation as well as the adjustment of thinking patterns.

The first and greatest thing to do if you are depressed is to reach out to others. While this goes against the stoic dogma of self-reliance, it is still an important tip that all modern psychotherapists extol. Staying connected with others will help to curtail depression by giving you an outlet to put forth your depressive thoughts and by ensuring that your peers will not abandon you in the future if you are a person who happens to have abandonment issues.

The next step towards dealing with depression is to do the things that you enjoy doing. This is not to advise blindly following any passions, as this would be adverse to the teachings of stoicism, but you should allow yourself to indulge in what you enjoy most to a certain extent when you are feeling depressed.

This step also involves doing the things that will protect the health of the body and of the mind. These things include getting lots of sleep (eight or more hours a day), managing stress effectively, practicing relaxation techniques, and eating well. You should also take note of what you enjoy the most and try to set aside more time for those activities.

Exercise is another extremely important mechanism of curtailing depression. It is the most repetitive exercises, however, that will always prove the most beneficial in this respect though. It would also be advisable here to add mindfulness practice of some sort to your daily schedule. This will reduce stress and make depressive symptoms much more manageable in the process.

Depression is one disorder that stoicism may often be wrongfully associated with. Many people confuse the indifference of the Stoics to pain and to joy with depression, which couldn't be more off base considering all that the stoic philosophy has to offer us in the way of combating depression.

Anxiety

Anxiety is one of the most harmful and prevalent negative emotions that plague modern people. A certain amount of anxiety is helpful as it fosters action in situations that call for it, but there is a fine line between anxiety that is helpful and anxiety that is damaging to our overall well-being. Here we should differentiate between short and long-term anxiety. Short term anxiety is more fight or flight response to problems within our immediate situations. This type of anxiety produces the hormone adrenaline, which comes from our adrenal glands. Long-term anxiety affects us throughout a much longer period of time and can have much more detrimental impacts on our overall health. The hormone most commonly associated with this type of anxiety is cortisol, a hormone produced also in our adrenal glands.

Our fight or flight response is the more useful of these two, considering that long-term anxiety often gives us much needless worry that ages us prematurely. This toll that excess long-term anxiety can take on us consists of troubles with concentrating, eating, and sleeping, in addition to many other health complications. Stoicism allows its most reliable antidote to long-term anxiety in its assertion that we should accept anxiety as a natural and helpful emotion to us.

Whether you suffer from only occasional and normal anxiety or you have a full-blown anxiety disorder, there are many things that you can do to combat anxious thoughts. The first step towards better managing your anxiety consists of taking a more realistic and objective glance at whatever it is that makes you anxious. This will allow you to better distinguish worries that are genuinely concerning from those that do not hold much merit. It is not only necessary here to take note of the relevance of an area of worry, but whether or not anything can be done to resolve its specific issue. If there is nothing in anyone's power that can be done to solve the issue, then it is not worth worrying about. Here stoicism has something to offer us in that multiple ancient Stoic philosophers warned against our dealing with issues that are without the boundaries of our power.

Next, we need to focus on challenging the negative thoughts that we find ourselves having. This is the very same point that Marcus Aurelius makes in his Meditations. In order to find better reasoning, we need to find a greater cosmic perspective on what goes on around us and to follow the logos or divine reason. Doing this will help shape our viewpoints into more healthy modes of thinking and lead to us making much clearer judgments and better decisions in the future.

Whenever we are confronted by a negative thought, one of the most important things that we can ask ourselves is whether or not this thought and or this thinking pattern at hand is beneficial to us. This should not be confused with asking whether or not it is true, as many true statements are simply irrelevant to us. If a thought is not helpful to us, then we should look instead for more helpful thoughts in the future.

Vanity

Vanity is one of the most prevalent negative personality characteristics that plague modern people. It is so easy to find oneself unable to get off of one's high horse when we find ourselves being assisted each and every day by our technology. We all need to step back from time to time however, in order to remind ourselves that our minds are usually capable of doing things that we are not always worthy of credit for and that whatever talents or characteristics we do have which make us feel proud should never be left up entirely for our own credit, because more often than not, we are standing on the shoulders of giants when it comes to doing what we are doing.

It is always much easier to recognize the vanity in others than to recognize the vanity in one's self. This vanity in others, however, can be used by us to determine what we should ourselves avoid in the way of our egos. Nearly all major religions and philosophies teach us that we are better off avoiding vanity at all costs and put constant checks on what our own egos will allow us to get away with.

Stoicism offers indifference to all of our personal accomplishments as well as our attributes, which may not make us feel very proud whenever it is that we achieve something great, but will always guard against our feeling being hurt whenever we fail. This also allows us to stop competing with all those around us and to just start living our lives like the personal architects that we truly are of ourselves.

Not only is vanity harmful in of itself, but it also causes lots of other characteristics that many would find unflattering in a person. These include but are not limited to shyness, boasting, gossiping, telling white lies, and relishing excessively in the inauthentic admiration of sycophants. From a Christian perspective, likely adopted from the Stoics, vanity can encourage sins against purity. This usually includes the exhaustion of sexual license in younger people who have yet to snap their egos into order.

From the Stoics themselves, we are taught to admit our faults and thinking errors regularly in order to move on from them, constantly adapting ourselves to new patterns of thought which may prove to be more beneficial to us. This involves, however, constant and repeated admission of ignorance which needs to be carried out throughout life. It is always easy to make the mistake of falling back into arrogant habits and thinking patterns. This is a practice which takes lots of time and energy to develop and does not show any immediate rewards to most, which is why the majority of people never take this up, but those who do are always made the better because of it.

Anger

Stoicism is one of the best philosophies for combating anger. Its teachings may apply better to those who have anger problems than any other types of people in that it constantly emphasizes the importance of staying calm and level-headed in all situations, a practice that is always especially helpful for the angriest among us. Not all of us are afflicted with excess anger or any temper management problems, but there are instances in all of our lives that push us past our own boiling points. Here, we should go over some of the most reliable methods of anger management which have been either put forth by or would be encouraged by the ancient Stoic philosophers.

The first tip regarding anger management is to be precise in your words. All too often, easily angered people also happen to be impulsive as well, which can shine through in the things that they say when angered. Focus on thinking actively about what you are about to say before saying it. This will prevent you from saying anything in a fit of anger that you may turn out to regret eventually.

The next tip is to only express your anger when you feel calm and are prepared to be mature about what is bothering you. If you blindly express your anger whenever you are not calm, then you are likely to make many lapses in judgment that you could have otherwise avoided. Try instead to give yourself time to gather your thoughts when provoked rather than laying everything out in the open where everyone can hear your own inner dialogues whether they want to or not. This comes with the ability to accept that you are simply not going to have all of the answers to your specific problems when first confronted with them. Next, it is important to get lots of exercise. This is not only an important step in managing anger, but it is important in managing your overall health and well-being. Stress reduction is also one of the most important benefits that exercise offers, which will, in turn, reduce overall anger.

Taking time to gather one's own thoughts and to come up with solutions to problems at hand is another incredibly important tip regarding anger management. All too often, people jump to conclusions about the things that provoke them without ever delving into any viable solutions to the problems that they are confronted with. Nearly all of the ancient Stoics advise against this and tell us that we need to focus on analyzing our problems objectively and applying all of our skills to solving them. While jumping to conclusions may provide immediate and sometimes satisfying solutions to our problems, it is only under further investigation into these problems that they can be solved effectively and their solutions related to other problems.

While anger may never be a flattering emotion, it is still a valid one nonetheless. The best way to deal with this emotion is neither to brush it aside nor to exalt it, but instead to analyze it carefully when it comes and to meet it with self-control.

Quick Start Action Step:

For your quick start action step, address a negative emotion you are currently experiencing and apply the stoic ideas presented in the previous section in order to help solve manage and even prevent the said negative emotion in the future.

Chapter 8: How to Thrive in a Stressful Environment

It is always the most stressful and uncomfortable situations that we are met with in life that define who we are the most. As far as normal situations in which we are put under a normal amount of pressure are concerned we often learn next to nothing and are not held accountable for proving who it is that we really are within these times. It is always the truly difficult and arduous tasks that we are met with that define our character and determine the trajectory of our lives instead.

When we find ourselves in situations that demand a lot out of us, we can feel the added pressure all the way down to a physiological level. In other words, it is not only our minds that are reacting to the stimulus but also our entire bodies, so it is no wonder to see how one event can determine our overall health for months or even years to come. Stoicism offers us a way of thinking that will enable us to come out of stressful situations with as much of our health intact as possible. This way of thinking involves meeting any tragedies or any stressful situations that we find ourselves in with equanimity to any of the great things that happen in our lives. While this equanimity may seem dull or prosaic to some, it still offers great strength when confronted with life's greatest adversities. When we divorce ourselves from the habit of meeting bereavement and agony with conclusion jumping and irrational decision-making, we gain the power to take on any tragedies that come our way relatively easily.

One question that we come to face with when confronted with adversity and discomfort is the question of how we should better comfort ourselves when under uncomfortable situations. It is when we are most out of our comfort zones that we need to be at our most observant and that we need to make ourselves feel as secure as possible. This is another point at which stoicism has a lot to offer us. Here the school encourages us to take a step back in moments of panic or crisis in order to give ourselves time to introspect and to analyze the situation at hand. This can be done most effectively by means of mindfulness practice, cold exposure (in relation to the thing and or situation which causes us anxiety), and regular exercise.

1) Mindfulness Meditation Practice

To start our discussion of these three methods, we will hear begin with mindfulness meditation practices. We should always keep in mind that the main objective of these practices is, in one way or another, to create some type of space for ourselves. This space should ideally be a space in which we feel at our most comfortable and secure. It takes lots of focus, energy, and practice to effectively obtain this space for ourselves, but once we have become accustomed to finding it there are great benefits to be found in doing so.

Within this aforementioned space, we can determine our reactions to the stimulus that we are confronted with, whatever it may be. This space remains our own and no one can intrude on to it, which makes our decision-making as far as our reactions are concerned left completely up to our own devices. No one else has the right or even the ability to influence the ways in which we respond to external stimuli. It is the ways in which we can manipulate our responses to these stimuli that determine the way that we are perceived by others and the way in which situations unfold involving us. This space that we create for ourselves is also very useful in that we can formulate the most appropriate possible responses to stimuli from stressful situations. This gives us lots of power regarding how to act when we don't know how to act. It is very easy, however, to jump to conclusions and plans without careful deliberation in times of crisis. In order to use this space to the best of our advantage, we need to practice mindfulness continually and attentively.

A fight or flight response is a body's most common reaction to some sort of stressful situation, which actually proves to be the worst possible reaction to these situations in a lot of scenarios. In order to best determine any courses of action within a stressful situation, we must take some time to deliberate our plans or reactions and see what our best responses would be. Fight or flight responses were evolved into the mechanisms of our ancestors in order to give them the incentive to run from our combat any predators that they may have come into contact with. There are, however, very few (if any) of these situations in the lives of most modern people, so these fight or flight responses are often assigned to situations in which we meet more mild forms of stress that are usually not life-threatening in any way. While the emotions that we may feel during these responses may sometimes overwhelm us we are always obligated to ourselves to control our actions throughout these times.

Mindfulness training involves not only determining how to respond to certain stimuli but also observing our initial and internal reactions to the stimuli in question. By observing these initial reactions (both physical and psychological), we can often get a better grasp of what we truly feel when these things happen. It is these initial reactions that are usually much rawer and therefore more telltale than are the conceptions that are later drawn from them. By observing and analyzing these reactions before we take time to strategize according to them, we can better understand how we react to certain situations, or in other words, what makes us tick and what doesn't.

There are many different methods of mindfulness meditation, all of which boast their own benefits and are beset by their own demerits. These include but are not limited to yoga, weight training, long distance running, and much more. Virtually any and all practices that engage our minds continually and force us to observe the happenings of our mind and body also work as great mindfulness training. In addition to finding the space for one's self which has already been gone over, mindfulness also consists of stepping outside of one's self as well. This usually involves, for a stoic perspective, connecting with that which is higher than the self and looking at happenings and situations from a viewpoint different than one's own. It is only with continued effort each and every day spanning quite some time that one can effectively learn mindfulness and use it to help them in his or her everyday life. In this way, mindfulness practice can help a person to transcend the happenings of their own stressful environment and instead focus on the happenings of their inner life, which is inexhaustible in its ability to be analyzed. This is not to be confused, however, with any forms of escapism. While it is important to detach oneself from stressful environments it remains equally important to keep up with the happenings of these environments in order to assure that one is never overwhelmed by anything that he or she has been missing.

2) Cold Exposure

Another great technique for overcoming stress in negative environments that also boasts many other benefits both cognitive and physical is that of exposure to cold temperatures. This is a practice that most people are not willing to take up themselves due to apprehension, but those who do receive great benefits including improved cardiovascular health and greater mental clarity, among many other things. The easiest and most common method of increasing cold exposure is to take cold showers.

Setting the water in one's shower at a lower temperature and continuing to shower in this manner on a daily basis will dramatically affect the trajectory of both your physical and mental lives. At first, the lowered temperature can seem overwhelming to some, but beyond a certain point, it becomes commonplace and hardly noticeable to shower at the lowered temperature. Not only will doing this provide better mental clarity, but it will also keep one used to being uncomfortable, another thing that stoic philosophy encourages continually. This ability will translate into greater flexibility and adaptability in every facet of one's life.

The natural responses that we have when taking cold showers are the same ones that we are met with in stressful situations and or environments. With this being said, we can learn to better control ourselves better in times of stress by exposing ourselves to cold regularly. If the abnormal and uncomfortable becomes normal and comfortable for us then we have nothing further to be apprehensive about facing.

In addition to fostering self-control, the act of exposing oneself to cold regularly also fosters self-discipline. When we stick to habits that we do not immediately enjoy we gain skills in controlling ourselves and in sticking to other habits that we are put off by. Desensitizing ourselves to the things that will help us eventually despite hurting us in the short term by our own estimations will make prioritizing our overall health seem much less daunting of a task than it would initially seem. Once we incorporate this self-discipline into our decision making within our everyday life, we become better able to weigh out options and come to conclusions more clearly and deliberately. This trait is also aided by the clarity of thought that the cold temperature provides in of itself.

Every time we overcome our urges to shower using hot water, we win an internal battle and build up our own fortification of decision making. This will train us to gain the ability to resist other potentially destructive forces in our lives, which is beneficial because often the key to success in modernity lies more in our resistance to certain things rather than or obtaining of certain things. We have mostly problems of plenty rather than of poverty, which is exactly the type of scenario that stoicism warns against.

3) Regular Exercise

Physically demanding work of any kind is another great way to thrive in a more stressful environment. Not only does this type of work have many obvious physical health benefits, but it also keeps the mind somewhat occupied when a person finds his or herself in a stressful environment. In addition to occupying the mind, exercise also provides the brain with excess oxygen, which is beneficial in terms of IQ because our brains need massive quantities of oxygen in order to function properly or to improve their functioning.

One other quality of physical exercise is that it usually involves a certain amount of pain. This pain is similar to the discomfort that we face during exposure to cold or any other thing that we are not familiar with or taxes us. We should make it a point throughout our lives to expose ourselves to pains just as we should expose ourselves at a young age to the chickenpox virus so that these issues do not do us under when they inevitably come up later. We tend to use our past experiences to judge our appropriate actions in the present, but here stoicism teaches us that we can avoid pain in our future by disregarding our comfort in the present.

The most simple and common type of exercise is most likely either walking or running, through weightlifting and playing sports or any sort are also great forms of exercise. It should be kept in mind that exercise of any sort should be practiced on a daily basis in order to achieve any substantial gains.

Mindfulness training, cold exposure, and physical activity are three of the most successful methods of combating stress in certain environments, but there are also some certain mindsets that should be kept while trying to do this as well. The first one of these that we should go over is a committal attitude. If you are not fully committed to doing everything in your power to reduce your stress then you are bound to keep the stress around until you fully commit to curtailing it.

We must first ascertain the full scope of what is brought into our attention before trying to commit to reducing all of our stress. If we are not taking note of what it is that we are surrounded by in the fullest detail possible than we can never be sure of what all we need to change within the situation. We should also determine what degrees of energy and attention are being spent on each particular item that we are spending our time on.

This commitment is not the fly by night type that at once vanishes as soon as things stop working in our favor. We have to stay committed to our goals no matter how murky the waters in our lives become and we have to be able and willing raft through whatever flood waters life has to throw at us. We cannot afford to withdraw during these periods of adversity either. It is always surprising just how much a person can be ostracized during and after a period of great hardship shared by all those around him or her, whether it is that person's fault or not. Staying connected with others not only ensures that we will not be abandoned in the future, but it also gives us a support group of some kind in the face of a crisis that we cannot face on our own. Whether or not we are being met with any type of hardship, however, we should still stay determined in all of our pursuits. There is simply no other way to accomplish a substantial task without persistent practice and hard work.

The next good mindset to keep when confronted with stressful situations or environments is a mindset of control. It is always important to build one's perspectives on external realities based on the mindset that we have some control or influence over those realities. Whether this is true or not it can give us a much more well-defined notion of power within our own lives. This perspective therefore gives us much more incentive to keep asserting our will onto the things that we perceive to be negative within our environments whenever things start to become hard to keep up with in our lives.

Feelings of being out of control are not only not very empowering but also very stressful to have, especially throughout a prolonged period of time. When people cannot see clearly all that they really are in control of within their lives they start to feel much better about where they are and also much more driven to get to somewhere even better. It fills people with ambition to know that they are in control of their own destinies, and they therefore pursue their own self-interest, which, as Adam Smith asserts, is usually in the best interest of society at large. Control is one mindset that can make any stressful situation feel like a walk in the park because those with this mindset are always in control of what happens around them.

Another mindset that is useful in stressful situations is one that allows that there is going to be a certain amount of challenge involved in whatever it is that life throws at us. The cost of existence itself is suffering- a tenet propounded by nearly every philosophical school in history, stoicism included. In order to control this suffering as much as possible, we must accept that it is permanent and address the issues that cause us stress as much as our own abilities will allow. If we continually address what is bothering us (which we are destined to do anyway) then we will eventually gain skill and confidence in our ability to do so. Gaining this confidence will come with the realization of some of our greatest powers and it will remind us that if we can face our own greatest demons then we will be able to truly do anything that we put ourselves up to.

From here we can start to set increasingly ambitious goals for ourselves and gain lots of skills in our endeavors to achieve these goals, whatever they may be. This does, however, involve searching through the unknown and working diligently towards what we want to do. This all requires lots of strength and courage, but there is simply no other way of getting oneself out of hard times and preventing oneself from being completely engulfed by the next flood that life will invariably have to offer.

Quick Start Action Step:

Select one of the strategies or mindset approaches found in this chapter to try, then see which works best for you that you can pursue and benefit from in the long term.

Chapter 9: How to Apply Stoicism in Relationships

While stoicism is often pigeonholed as something of an antisocial mode of being, there do remain lots of benefits in stoicism regarding developing healthier relationships that many modern people and their proclivity towards oversharing would be wise to take upon themselves. Seneca encourages both the mental practice of writing certain things that we do not need or want in our lives off and the practice of preparing preemptively for the loss of certain things while they are still with us so that we are prepared when they leave us. Both practices can be applied to the people we know as well, and often should in a lot of cases.

One truism that most people do not want to accept for themselves is the fact that we are not obligated to keep those in our lives who we do not enjoy being around. All too often people stay in relationships with others who they cannot stand to be around simply because they fear isolation or are not secure enough to face the chaos of life alone. It is also common that people settle or pretend to enjoy the company of others because they can find no one else to spend time with themselves.

This practice of considering all that we are going to one day be missing is very similar to considering our own mortality in that it connects us at once with what is most important to us and what we should stay motivated to do with our lives. This practice also reminds us that we should show more gratitude for all that we have in the present moment. Often times we are not able to clearly see what is most important in our lives while we are busy going about our usual business. Taking time to reconnect with our mortality and the finitude of the things and people around us reminds us of what we would want our last moments to be spent doing and what we would are currently taking for granted in life.

There is one anecdote in particular passed on down to us by Seneca that illustrates the stoic viewpoint on tragedy and how to face it virtuously. In this anecdote, a stoic by the name of Stilbo has had his town sacked and family slaughtered by barbarians while away from home. When Stilbo returned home he was asked what he had lost to which he replied that he had lost nothing, continuing that his goods were still with him.

This response may seem cold by most estimates, but it is in line with what the Stoics taught as far as apatheia is concerned. To the Stoics, apatheia is the state of being completely undisturbed by any and all lesser emotions that we may feel such as petty annoyances and frivolous passions. The word apatheia should not be confused here with the English word *apathy* as its translation in reality is closer to the word equanimity than any other word, equanimity in these cases meaning something similar to contentment.

While in a state of apatheia we are not directed by any lesser passions that may come to our mind. Here we accept the fact that we are going to face tribulations and hardships and know that these happenings are just as necessary to us as are any positive happenings. As far as handling any future losses is concerned, the key to doing so with apatheia is to value properly and be grateful for the things and people that we do have in the present moment. Taking this step now will prevent us from feeling like we did not appreciate what we may have had when we had it.

Keeping a mindset of apatheia frees us up considerably in that we feel free from needs or wants when we have released petty emotions from our hearts and minds. It is only once we have reduced or needs to near zero that we can feel truly free in life. So long as we want or own things, we will have things that we cannot obtain and other things that can be taken away from us. This puts us in a position or constant worry and strife over things that do not bring us any joy, akin to slavery. This is what we would call a minimalist perspective today that many would do very well to adopt for themselves. Even in the times of the ancient Stoic philosophers, it was a virtue to be scrupulous. It still is today, though many people and interests would rather you believe otherwise.

Attaining apatheia, while it may seem rather easy, is a surprisingly hard thing to accomplish. We can never genuinely determine the value of everything that we are presented with in the present, so trying to do so comes with a fair bit of trial and error, naturally. This goal of achieving complete indifference to all of our lesser emotions which most people are so absorbed in is a very lofty one, but there is one thing here that should be said about lofty goals: they drive us to loftier feats of personal accomplishment.

When we push ourselves towards accomplishing more demanding goals, we, in the process, do one of two things or both; we redefine what impossible is for ourselves and or we accomplish the goal at hand. As you can tell, whether we meet our goals in these scenarios we always get a great reward of one type or another. It is only once we have made ourselves accustomed to aiming towards high goals that we can get over our fears of lofty tasks.

Those genuinely pursuant of the ideal state of apatheia are usually met with more reward than they ever initially imagine they could obtain. The pursuit of this state is so rewarding because it involves our meeting the challenges of every day with the same level-headed indifference that we met those of the previous day with. It is blissful to remain in a state of apatheia because it frees us from all of the strife that we would otherwise subject ourselves to. Persistence here is key though. If we are not constantly pursuing this state than it will become more elusive than it would be otherwise.

It is only when we are consistently struggling to better ourselves that we can look back on our past with contentment. If we are not making continued progress from the present to the future in the way of improving ourselves then we can never expect to have a good future, a good present, or be able to look back on our past with any greater joy.

Apatheia is not only a state that should be pursued in one's own inner life, however. This is also a state that should be pursued within intrapersonal relationships as well. The two main practices which are of most help in trying to apatheia within a relationship are curiosity and growth. Applying these two practices within conversations usually has a way of starting up better conversations, promoting more meaningful conversation topics, and prevents the wasting of time in unproductive arguments.

Curiosity should always be genuine, in other words, questions shouldn't be forced and meaningless, but instead it always better to ask only what we really want to be answered. What usually stands in the way of asking well thought out questions for most people is the problem of ego. This is said because most of the fears that surround the asking of hard questions have to do with ego: the fear of saying something foolish, or being wrong, etc. He, as anywhere, we will do very well to leave our ego out of conversations, and our thinking patterns, for that matter.

To better understand just how seldom it is that people take a genuine interest in the lives of others we only need to think of when the last time was that we were asked questions about our dreams, aspirations, or long-term goals was. This time was more than likely quite a while ago because most never take interests in these subjects. This is why it makes such a long-lasting impression on us when we are asked about these things. We remain grateful for the opportunities to speak on these subjects for life because we spend so much time wanted to have interest taken in us and rarely have the privilege of having that happen.

Without genuine curiosity taken in another person, no real empathy can be developed and no long-lasting connections can be made. If one of the first presuppositions about another person that comes into our mind is that the person is somehow boring and dull and we do not adopt this presupposition to meet whatever is interesting about him or her then we are missing out on a great opportunity to learn a lot from another person's life and perspective. We cannot expect to create meaningful bonds that continually engage and inspire us without some efforts made toward taking further interests in those who we are talking to on our parts.

Curiosity also prevents us from fostering prejudices. If we take more of an interest in another person than we are bound to find that they are somewhat similar to us and that most of the issues that we may with him or her are rather trivial and or fly by night. Our minds also gain creativity when we are taking an interest in another person or thing. Inquiring into someone or something forces us to think outside of the box and to problem solve in ways that we would have otherwise never come up with.

Curiosity also makes us use resources that we would have never even come across otherwise. The most interest that we take in something or someone else, the more we learn overall through anecdotes, facts, etc. This also helps us to push through hard times more easily, as all additional information that we have usually does.

When mixed with some form of personal growth is when curiosity starts to really help us the most. While curiosity alone, without the addition of growth made, may offer us some temporary satisfaction, it usually (if not always) leads to pain in the long term. These periods that involve no personal growth are always looked back on by us with some sense of disappointment at not having used the time to our best advantage.

If we are growing but not developing our curiosity then we are bound to find some sort of satisfaction in life, but we are still missing out on lots of opportunities to learn more things from our surroundings. This mindset is also hurtful in that it does not allow for any ambiguity in our actions, or in other words, we put blinders on and go about performing only what we are predetermined to rather than ever looking for other avenues by which we can learn and experience new things.

It is the admixture of both growth and curiosity that leads to both meaning and satisfaction in our lives in the long term. Combining these two traits is the only way of ensuring that we lead the most fulfilling life possible and that the journeys that we find ourselves going on are always pleasurable to look back on. Stoicism allows us, through the state of apatheia, to delve into our present with these practices fearlessly and uninhibited. This admixture is also ideal for building relationships overall because it allows us to look forward to our future with another person and also enjoy the present spent with him or her.

When we look towards a goal of maintaining apatheia we start to see a more enlightening view of our own mortality and we therefore prioritize how we are spending our life presently differently, making much more progress in our lives, usually.

Most people are remiss to put the practices of growth and curiosity into action when forming relationships because doing so takes immense faith and some degree of vulnerability on the practitioner's part. This also involves a fair bit of uncertainty, which is something that all too many people are usually afraid to face.

Stoicism encourages us to consistently admit our ignorance to ourselves, which in turn makes facing uncertainty much easier for us because we start to see it as a natural part of our condition. This makes it a lot easier to practice growth and curiosity in our relationships because we are assured that whatever happens, we will just continue to grow and to learn more. It is very important that we never give up on the pursuit of knowledge and or growth even when these things might seem to be at their most elusive. If we cease to use our faculties to determine what it is that we need to know or do next then we are bound to suffer greatly and to remain ignorant of what the true purposes are or can be.

Ignorance is the only reliable precursor to growth that we have in life. When in a state of apatheia we accept that we do not know everything and continue on our path to intellectual and spiritual growth regardless. We can only find meaningful memories in the ways in which we are pursuing greater knowledge in life. When we are not focused on growing and are not curious about anything then we do not have meaning in our lives, regardless of whatever may be happening to or around us.

It is only the culmination of knowledge gained throughout periods of uncertainty that make up our greater knowledge base. This is primarily due to the fact that we are simply less motivated to look for new knowledge throughout the periods in which there is no uncertainty.

It should also be mentioned that it takes personal growth of some sort to build better relationships, after all, why would anyone want to spend time around another person who is not interested in even developing him or herself? What does such a person have to offer anyone else if he or she is offering nothing to their self? In addition, it takes all parties within a relationship working toward apatheia to make any difference or progress with others.

Quick Start Action Step:

Begin by applying a concept mentioned on this chapter that would help improve your relationship with others. Take note of the outcome as a result and work towards getting more positive outcomes in future opportunities.

Bonus Chapter: Stoicism and Mindfulness

Both Stoicism and Buddhism preach the same philosophy regarding living in the present moment. Therefore, when practicing mindfulness, it would be beneficial to study the works of the ancient Stoics, as well as many Buddhist philosophers. Marcus Aurelius once noted that each and every one of us lives only in the present moment and that anything in the past has already been lived while anything in the future remains uncertain. Thich Nhat Hanh also encouraged living in the present when he noted that one's attention should only be drawn to the present because we can only be sure of living in the present.

Both Buddhism and stoicism teach that each and every hour that we are working on tasks we should devote our time and energy chiefly to the task at hand, leaving no room for distractions or side projects of any sort. This is a great practice to use to avoid getting scatterbrained and overwhelmed by the multitude of tasks that each of us is assigned with every day of our lives. Doing this also makes us much better performers in whatever it is that we are doing. When the mind is unhindered by multiple tasks it has a way of zeroing in more effectively on the singular task at hand, creating more focus and attention.

The practice mentioned above is one very similar to mindfulness training.

Mindfulness training discourages any and all multitasking and instead encourages us to work at our own pace, starting from the bottom up to achieve our goals. One later philosopher, Descartes, would extol the virtues in dividing up the issues that we are met with into their smallest components and working our way from the easiest tasks within them to the hardest ones. Epictetus calls this Focus attention and teaches his students that using this attention is one of the keys to living an ethical life. He also proclaims that this attention can not only be used when completing large tasks, but should also be used throughout the completion of any tasks, and even throughout our free time.

Epictetus even goes so far as to proclaim that this attention is our most natural state of mind. He asserts that whenever our minds go wandering and have to therefore be put back in place through attention, we have diverged from the state at which our mind should stay in the first place. Here Epictetus' attention becomes a fundamental part of the stoic creed. Buddhism also offers a similar tenant to us: a father or a mother can never do as much for a person as the even directional of his or her mind.

Most modern conceptions of mindfulness meditation are similar to the ones practiced in Buddhism, but not the ones practiced by stoics. The Buddhists are famous for their monks, mountain temples, and meditation practices, why the Stoics have little to no common imagery surrounding them within the public imagination. Here it would be beneficial to delve into some of the basics of stoic mindfulness training because this sort of mindfulness training is often overshadowed in the modern world by other sorts.

The attention that Epictetus teaches us to use is best applied to ethical concepts within everyday scenarios, or better, how to use ethics to our advantage pragmatically with in our everyday lives. Here knowing ethics is only useful if we also know how to use these ethical practices for the benefit of us and those around us regularly. The first thing to know now is that we are only trying to influence the things that are within our control and not wasting our energy on things that are not. And now we are presented with the question: are we things that are entirely within our own control, or do we really influence our own being, and to what extent, if so? This is one of the basic fundamental questions of free will which is been asked repeatedly throughout philosophical history.

The difference between places and situations in which we are in control and in which we are not is another very subtle one with very determinant implications. Whether or not another person approves of us, for example, can have a greater impact then we like to imagine within our own lives. Disapproval is at once out of our control and detrimental to us, while approval is out of our control and beneficial to us. We can control neither of these, which brings both of them into the realm of the uncertain, which stoicism teaches us that we should accept and live with.

We are constantly basing our own actions off of what we can infer should be done about things that are in and out of our control. We should obviously do more about what is in our control, but there should also be some energy invested in fixing things that are out of our control. This energy should be limited only to the things that have the most detrimental impacts on us because even this energy will likely go to waste as we cannot control what we are trying to for certain.

Typically, it is only the things that are out of our control that will give us anxiety, so we should usually focus only on things that are within our control. Putting too much energy into trying to change things that we cannot definitively change usually leads to more suffering than is necessary. We should also avoid being desirous of things that we cannot control. this inevitably and invariably causes disappointment and jealousy towards those who have what we want. We can only count on getting the things that are within our powers to get, these things are necessary to us, while everything outside of our powers is contingent.

As far as other people's reactions to what we do are concerned, let's take a pianist for example. A pianist who is seeking nothing but fame and admiration it's going to be disappointed if he or she is not met with applause at a performance. A stoic pianist, on the other hand, will always be more interested in the music itself than in any external reaction to it. This gives the stoic pianist power over the other in that the stoic pianist is not basing his or her own self-perception of the music on whether or not it was met with applause from the audience. Another benefit of stoicism in this example is the performance benefit, a performer who is focused primarily on the quality of the music is more likely to play great music and therefore gain more applause than the performer who, profligate for applause, neglected to master the music that he or she was playing. Here, has anywhere, it proves to be more important to focus on the task at hand than any external realities that we do not have much control over, the external reality in this case being the applause or lack thereof of the audience.

One of the greatest questions that we can ask ourselves when practicing stoic mindfulness is the question of what role we are trying to fill within the situations that we find ourselves in. Epictetus taught his students that if they were to find themselves in a role in which they had no real power, they should have reminded themselves to step away from the role. The number one rule of Game Theory, on a related note, is that we should never play strictly dominated games. Another rule of Game Theory is that we should itinerantly delete any dominated games. Here are dominated games would be the situations in which we have no power. To be effective game theorists we must not involve ourselves in situations such as these.

Pulling ourselves away from situations that we have no influence over not only saves us lots of energy and suffering, but it also allows us to sharpen our skill sets regarding what we can influence. We simply cannot make very much improvement in the areas that we should if we are investing much of our time and energy into things that are out of our control.

Some of stoicism's greatest opponents argue that stoic mindfulness training leads to selfishness because it encourages those who practice it to think only about is things that they can influence, excluding all other things. This practice is, however, not as solipsistic as these opponents would have most believe. The aim that stoic mindfulness training teaches, virtue above pettiness, works to the benefit of the greater good when it is aimed at by individuals. it should also be argued that we cannot serve the interests of others properly until we have served our own interests to a certain extent. So, whether or not our own personal interests benefit others, it is always more beneficial for everyone to pursue their own interests before trying to be charitable toward others.

Buddhism teaches us that all forms of possessiveness are an evil in of themselves because they lead to greed and profligation. The Stoics, on the other hand, believe that possessiveness is only a destructive force when we are covenant over things that we have no control over. Wanting these things that we cannot influence is an easy gateway towards unlimited suffering because these wants that we have will rarely, if ever, be met.

Here Epictetus teaches us to make the distinction between wants of our moral purpose and wants of our externals. we can only hope to fulfill the wants of our moral purpose, which is only found within us because we are the only things that we ultimately control. It follows as a corollary that only the wants of our moral purpose can even benefit us. Our wants of externalities can not only not be expected to be met, but they usually don't even benefit us when they are met.

Stoicism can replace selfishness with altruism by teaching us that our own actions are in our control. We can choose to be benevolent, generous, and sincere to others, which the Stoics believed people naturally were. It is within our nature to be communal and to cooperate with others, which is why if we are left to our own devices for serving our own self-interests, we will be inclined naturally to do good unto others. It would necessarily follow that malevolence is foreign to human nature and that it can be due to petty egoism and greed, both of which practicing stoic mindfulness can and will curtail.

While focusing only on what is up to us in our lives may seem limiting to our powers, it's actually usually extremely empowering to better understand just how much influence we have over our own destinies and the happenings that take place among us. Stoic mindfulness teaches us to go about asserting our will on the things that we can in an altruistic and benevolent manner so far as possible. 20th-century Russian composer Igor Stravinsky used to proclaim that it was only by limiting himself to the things that immediately demanded his attention that he was able to get as far in life as he got. we would all be wise to take this man's advice, especially in today's world where it is so easy to allow ourselves to be distracted by the constant input of information and obligation that we are bombarded with. Stoic meditation limits us, but in limiting us it gives us so much more power over our own lives.

Now we should bring ourselves back to Epictetus' term attention. this term can be applied in a number of ways. It can mean to pay attention to something, to be in an attentive mental state, or it can mean that we are focusing on one thing more so than any other thing. This term can apply to attention used in more mindful States as well as attention used and more hectic States. It is attention used in more mindful states, however, that we should focus on here.

Whether we are attentive of things that are in or outside of our power, we should only act on those things which we can control. While we should maintain attentiveness towards everything that we come into contact with as much as our powers allow, we should reserve our actions for things that we can actually influence generally. It would then follow here that we would naturally pay more attention to the things that we can control and that are in immediate contact with us.

It is when this stoic conception of attention is applied in tandem with other stoic conceptions such as logic and or divine reason that we can start to see great benefits in our thinking and in our lives. If we follow the divine reason and apply our undivided attention to what this reason may be telling us to do, we can start to more easily determine what steps we should take in the present to improve on our situations. If we do not assign our greatest attention to the divine reason and we will not have our path as clearly delineated as it could otherwise be.

The Stoic conception of logic is a propositional one that is heavily dependent upon the connections between things and ideas. Following these connections can make us more easily see the workings of divine reason and more easily apply our attention to our external reality. The working through of this propositional logic involves a fair amount of guess and check as well as the stripping away of many of our presuppositions. This process is naturally accompanied by a great deal of uncertainty, which stoicism teaches us to embrace. While working with this propositional system of logic, we can clear up our thinking and better determine the interconnectedness of the world around us.

Attentiveness, in stoicism, usually applies to the observation of one's own thoughts and actions, although it can also necessarily apply to anything else in or out of our control. While examining our own inner workings as well as the workings of our external reality it would be very beneficial for us to also observe the practices of Stoic logic and following the divine reason. This tripartite system of thinking will not only teach us a lot about ourselves and the world initially but will also clear up our thinking patterns for further learning of these things in the future.

Bonus Book Preview:

Enneagram Self-Discovery: Easy-to-Follow Essential Guide on How to Uncover your Unique Path with the 9 Enneagram Personality Types to Build Self-Awareness and Achieve Personal Growth by: Morgan Christopher Hudson

Chapter 1: Getting Started with Enneagram Personality Types

You may have heard of the Enneagram personality types from a friend or a co-worker. Maybe you heard about it in another book, at religious practices, on television, or at work. Whatever piqued your interest on the Enneagram personality types, you can use them to benefit you through all aspects of life.

You can grow stronger as a person and become more balanced. But first, what is the Enneagram method? If you heard about it elsewhere, it may have seemed complex. But don't worry. You will learn all about Enneagram here in a straightforward and enjoyable process!

In psychology, the human mind, consciousness, and unconsciousness combine to form what is known as the human psyche. It is believed that the nine personality types in the Enneagram method are closely tied to the human psyche. Because of this, we all have one of these nine types as the main point in our personality from birth. This impacts our temperament and dominant personality traits.

This personality type that we have from birth is known as our dominant type. While it is possible to have multiple types, one will usually be dominant. This is especially true during childhood.

This dominant personality type will influence our emotions, thoughts, and behavior as a child. This process shapes our entire childhood and influences who we become as adults.

Although you may see yourself in several different types, maybe even all of them, you will have one main type. This is the type that influences you the most throughout your life. This type is the most important for you to understand to gain control and balance over your life.

Talking with other people of the same Enneagram type as yourself, you may be confused. After all, this person seems to be completely different from you! But this does not mean that you or they were mistakenly typed. In fact, while people of the same type will share certain characteristics, they can be quite different as well. Our mental health, fears and anxieties, and life experiences can cause us to be different, even if we are the same type as another person.

Our individualistic traits might also be impacted by some of the other types. For instance, if you are a type Five, then you could have many traits of type Four or type Six. This is because these two types are directly next to the Five and share some commonalities. These types are known as your wing types, and they help you to remain balanced.

The personality types in order of One to Nine are the Reformer, the Helper, the Achiever, the Individualist, the Investigator, the Loyalist, the Enthusiast, the Challenger, and the Peacemaker.

You may now understand the most basic aspects of the Enneagram method, but everything has a story. Just like everything else, this is true for the Enneagram personality types and their origins.

The Enneagram method and personality types have a long and rich history from a myriad of ancient traditions and wisdom. All of these beautiful insights from ancient cultures were combined by the Bolivian Oscar Ichazo. Along with being raised in his home country of Bolivia, Ichazo spent much time in Peru during his childhood. However, as an adult, he moved to Argentina. This is where he studied at a school of inner work. His studies at this school would shape him and inspire him to create the Enneagram method. In fact, soon after he completed his studies at this school, he traveled to Asia. While there, he continued his studies on culture, religion, and a person's very being. After Asia, Ichazo journeyed to South America. This is when he first began to write down the Enneagram methods and types by using everything he had learned from around the globe.

Then, in the late '60s and early '70s, Ichazo officially created the Arica School. The purpose of this school was to be a school of knowledge, which has traditionally been employed by the Greek, Buddhists, Sufi, and Hindu to provide enlightenment. It became a school with deep and interwoven teachings focusing on spirituality, cosmology, psychology, metaphysics, and more.

Well-known psychologists and writers have even visited the Arica School such as John Lilly and Claudio Naranjo. While there, they were able to learn Ichazo's methods of self-realization firsthand. Lilly and Naranjo were taught the fundamentals of the system and even engaged in their practices.

Many people incorrectly believe that George Gurdjieff was the one to develop the Enneagram method and the corresponding nine personality types.
This is because the ancient symbol of the Enneagram, as shown in the image, had been lost in modern society. However, the symbol that is the foundation of the Enneagram personality method was reintroduced into society by Gurdjieff at his own school of inner work, which was highly influential. He would teach the symbol of the Enneagram through a series of movements and dances. The purpose of this was to give his students a profound

sense of meaning for the symbol and that which it represents.

Yet, it is clear that Gurdjieff did not teach his students the personality types and their method, as Ichazo did. The only teaching close to the personality types that Gurdjieff taught was the Chief Feature. He described this as being the characteristics that most define a person, their ego. But, unlike Ichazo, Gurdjieff used the Sufi method to communicate their Chief Feature. He would do this by telling the person what their most prominent faults were.

Due to this, many people early on mistakenly believed that it was George Gurdjieff who began the Enneagram personality method. This led to a widespread misunderstanding for decades on who the true originator actually was. While the method may have been inspired by a number of religions, it was Ichazo who combined all of the knowledge with the Enneagram method and first taught it.

There may be helpful personality typing

systems that have a number of various types, most commonly three, four, or sixteen. But, the Enneagram method is different from these types at a foundational level.

Rather than being a simple list of various personalities, the Enneagram system is based on holistic symmetry and mathematics. This simple yet detailed design uses lines to represent the ways that energy can move in patterns.

When this ancient diagram is applied to people, it shows that we have many psychological patterns that can be revealed by the lines of the Enneagram.

By using this ancient symbol, Ichazo was able to further examine the human soul. More specifically, he found ways in which our soul and thinking becomes distorted, affecting our ego. When developing his theories about this, he greatly relied on Western philosophies. One of the most prominent of these philosophies was the idea of nine divine forms discussed by Plato in Platonic Solids or The Divine Forms.

Through Ichazo's development of this method, we have been able to learn that the Enneagram is an intertwining of lines that can move and influence us. By following these lines, we can further discover the interactions and influences that we can expect from other personality types within the system. While we are born with a main or dominant type which remains constant, we are able to be pushed or pulled along the lines of the Enneagram. Once we have moved along the lines, we can experience a significant change in our point of view or perspective. We may become able to respond to situations and the world around us in new ways we previously wouldn't have. This means that the lines can help us further explore our psyche. Through the lines, we can learn more about ourselves and find a new sense of balance and development.

It's understandable to be skeptical of the Enneagram method. After all, it's a mystery to us how it is able to predict people's behavior. Most of us are uninterested in New Age beliefs with no scientific proof. But, just because the

Enneagram method is once again gaining attention doesn't mean that it is New Age mumbo-jumbo. Don't believe me? What's the harm in testing out this method in your own life? You will soon see the results and benefits. You don't have to take my word for it, you can take it into your own hands. Hundreds of thousands of people long before you have received benefits from using the Enneagram method within their own lives, and it is now your turn.

We recently mentioned that there are a number of different personality typing systems. That raises the question, how does the Enneagram personality method compare to one of the most hyped personality tests, the Myers-Briggs (MBTI) method?

There are various foundational differences between the two types. One of these is the distinction of nature versus nurture and their effects on a person's personality. While these systems teach that both nature and nurture have an effect on a person, they teach them in different ways and their opinion on these aspects differ.

Neither Myers-Briggs or C. Jung who was influential in its creation discussed or wrote on the subject of nurture on more than a rare occasion. They taught that our personalities are largely nature, something that we are born with. Whereas they believed nurture was simply a compensation to help us manage in society. For instance, an introvert may learn to compensate in situations that are largely extroverted.

While the Enneagram method also teaches that we are born with our personality types by nature, they largely emphasize the effects that nurture has upon our psyche. Looking back on your childhood, you may be able to see how certain events and the way they impacted who you are today. This is how nurture affects us.

When discussing our psychological health, both methods of personality typing have something to say.

With MBTI, it is believed that people have both

prominent and inferior functions. This could mean that someone is more feeling than analytical or vice versa. But, some people may behave unknowingly repressing their "inferior" function, which is needed in order to be whole.

On the other hand, with the Enneagram method, you can learn your propensity for specific core vices, which impact your choices and reactions. This may mean that you are more prone to pride, envy, or another vice. But by learning what vice you are most prone to, you can learn to become more balanced.

Myers-Briggs may tell you how you think, take in information, and make decisions. But unlike the Enneagram method, it doesn't help you understand how you feel and why. MBTI may tell you what career you are most suited for, but it doesn't ask what motivates you the most or what causes your stress the most. Yet, with Enneagram, you can learn the answers to these questions and more about yourself. You can learn things about yourself that you never recognized before.

Knowing ourselves is the key to changing and improving. We all have behaviors that become automatic. These can affect both ourselves and those around us. These behaviors may affect small day-to-day choices, or they could impact large life-changing choices. Either way, if we don't know ourselves, then we will remain stagnant and unbalanced.

The Enneagram personality method can show us the areas we are most likely to make mistakes, where we might get stuck, routine behaviors that we are oblivious to, and what's the biggest fear lying deep within our hearts might be.

Although, it doesn't only show the negative. The Enneagram can help push us forward, give us a deeper understanding to ourselves, increase our understanding and compassion towards others, help us to let go of damaging behaviors and patterns, and overall become the person that we want to be.

Rather than a static cookie cutter personality

type, the Enneagram is a tool that shifts and flows as we do. By using this tool throughout our lives, we can reach our full potential, learn to use our inherent gifts, and fully engage in a life worth living. This process is often known as increasing our emotional intelligence, and it not only benefits ourselves but everyone around us.

The three main components of emotional intelligence are:

1. Having an emotional awareness of ourselves, where we can both identify and name our own emotions.

2. The ability to harness our emotions and apply them to various tasks such as solving a problem.

3. Managing emotions, both by being able to regulate our own and by having the ability to either calm down or cheer up those around us.

As you can see, emotional intelligence is a simple concept, which we need to use on a daily basis. But just because the concept is simple doesn't mean it is actually simple to use. That is if we haven't been taught or aren't aware of how to harness or increase our emotional intelligence.

Some of the ways that having a higher emotional intelligence level may help you include:

- **You learn to better help others**
  One of the best ways we can impact the lives of others is by genuinely helping them. You may have many academic and professional accomplishments, but what will really impact a person is whether or not you are willing to help them. By learning to better help people, you can inspire them and build a more trusting relationship.

- **You can sincerely apologize**
  When we are too prideful to admit to even small mistakes and especially the big ones, then the people around us take notice. They begin to trust us less and

will feel pushed away. But when we gain a better understanding of ourselves, we are able to apologize with courage and strength. By showing humility, people will feel more comfortable and drawn toward you.

- **You can be authentic**
  Some people inaccurately believe that being authentic means that you share every part of yourself and your life to everyone. But this is a misconception brought about by lacking emotional intelligence. In truth, being authentic means that you truly believe what you say. That you stick to your principles and values. Not everyone appreciates authenticity. But in our technological age where it is difficult to tell truth from lie and friend from foe, being authentic is greatly valued.

- **Connect more**
  Having empathy means that we are able to understand others' feelings and thoughts. Rather than labeling or

judging people, we can begin to see the world through their eyes. By doing this, we can not only better connect with those in our own lives, but people around the world.

This doesn't mean you will always agree with a person, but you can deepen your understanding of them.

This is only a taste of what the Enneagram method can help you with. If you want to truly invest in your life and the lives of others, this book can help. But you can't simply read this book, you have to act on it. Purposefully learn your Enneagram personality type and practice self-awareness.

If you would like to learn more about the Enneagram method continue reading. You can also schedule time into your week to follow this chapter's Quick Start Action Step to learn more about the basics of the method.

Your Quick Start Action Step:

This book has everything you need to understand the basics of the Enneagram method, learn more about your personality type, become increasingly balanced, and more. But that doesn't mean that there aren't other helpful resources out there as well. Check out these links in order to deepen your understanding of the Enneagram method!

- https://www.enneagraminstitute.com
- https://www.reddit.com/r/Enneagram/

Chapter 2: Discovering Your Enneagram Personality Type

If you don't know where to begin when looking for an Enneagram test or how to interpret the results, don't worry. In this chapter, you will learn all you need to know to have confidence when choosing a test and reading the results.

Firstly, it is important to know that there are a lot of tests out there that were created by anyone off the street, just like those Facebook quizzes that tell you what type of pizza you are. These tests are inaccurate and will be unable to help you find your true Enneagram personality type. But don't worry! At the end of this chapter, in the Quick Start Action Step, I will provide you with an accurate test you can use.

There are many tests out there that will ask if you disagree, strongly disagree, somewhat agree, strongly agree, or are neutral. Each of the responses adds a point to a specific personality type or two, which is then added to your total. These tests are the most common because they are the easiest to create with the software available. These tests are usually not created by anyone accredited or even by someone anonymous. You are unlikely to get an accurate result out of these tests. If yours does happen to be accurate, it is most likely because these tests can't always be wrong. Statistically, they must be right on a rare occasion. But even if they are right, you won't know if you haven't taken an accurate test.

Some people will simply try to read through a list of traits that are common with the nine types to discover their individual personality type. The reason this is unreliable is that these descriptions can vary greatly depending on how the writer interpreted the characteristics. Not only that, but the traits and characteristics of the types may not fit a person one-hundred percent. This can lead a person to believe that they aren't their true personality type.

The method used by the most accurate test will force you to choose between one of two statements. Even if you don't feel strongly either way, you will have to figure out which option you slightly more toward. Think about it as if the eye doctor is asking you if options one or two are better. You may not be sure what the difference between the two lenses is, but you have to choose one of them.

At the end of the test, your score is added up and you can see a list of all of the types in order of how you scored on them. Most likely your highest score is your dominant type. But for people who are closely tied to two or three types, their dominant type may actually be one of the other types that they scored highly on.

You will score the highest on one of the following types:

- Type One: The Reformer
- Type Two: The Helper
- Type Three: The Achiever
- Type Four: The Individualist
- Type Five: The Investigator
- Type Six: The Loyalist
- Type Seven: The Enthusiast
- Type Eight: The Challenger
- Type Nine: The Peacemaker

When taking the official Enneagram test, it is usually rather obvious what your dominant personality type is. This is because your dominant type will most likely score three or four points higher than any of the other personality types. You can then confirm the type by reading over the personality's characteristics and traits, determining if they fit.

To learn more about this book and how it can help improve your personal growth, visit the online store and type in "Enneagram Self Discovery Morgan Christopher Hudson" in the search box.

Conclusion

Thank you for making it through to the end of *Stoicism for Beginners: How to Apply Ancient Stoic Wisdom Today using Practical and Simple Steps to Overcome Obstacles, Attain Contentment and Live a Better Life.*

Let's hope that this book was as helpful and as informative as possible. It should not be thought that since you have finished this book you now have nothing else to learn on the subject. the next step in better knowing and practicing the tenets of stoic philosophy would be to study the works of the ancient stoic philosophers further and to apply their teachings to your everyday life. It should be kept in mind that stoic philosophy is a lifestyle and not just some temporary fixation. It follows that practicing stoic philosophy is something that needs to be developed over time consistently.

One of the primary tenets of stoic philosophy is the fostering of self-knowledge. This fostering consists of being honest with ourselves regarding our ignorance and our limitations, among other things.

To make better stoics out of ourselves, we must accept the fact that we really do not know as much as we think we know.

After this step has been taken—and only after—we can start to perceive the world around us more clearly through a new, uninhibited optic that will lead us to more valuable knowledge and a better outlook in life.

www.ingramcontent.com/pod-product-compliance
Lightning Source LLC
Chambersburg PA
CBHW051547020426
42333CB00016B/2138